REBEL BAKES

REBEL BAKES

George Hepher

80+ Deliciously Creative Cakes,
Bakes + Treats For Every Occasion

greenfinch

CONTENTS

HOB JOBS

COOKIES + TARTS

AFTER-DINNER SINNERS

CAKE IT 'TIL YOU MAKE IT

Well lemme tell you something because I first started George's Bakery after a few months of horizontal ineptitude – a brief sabbatical from responsibilities – in 2015.

It all started when my mother, we call her Lady Jayne, told me to find something I was good at, and baking was the first thing that sprang to mind. You see, I was never a fan of my mum's meals growing up so at a young age, I started cooking on the weekends, and finding time to bake my favourite recipes from our tatty and crumbling Be-Ro recipe book was always the height of fun. And so my passion for baking was born.

With a relaxed approach to making money but the desire for a stately home, I applied to trade at my local farmers' market in 'the other St Ives' in Cambridgeshire. (The main differences are that St Ives in Cambridgeshire has an even older median age and a less impressive body of water – I implore everybody to voyage on a Great River Ouse Booze Cruise.) After a few years of baking in my parents' kitchen, I slowly grew (read: was pushed) out into a glorified granny shed where I baked for up to 20 hours a day to create enough stock for two more local farmers' markets in Ely and Cambridge. I carried on like that until the council wanted to kick me out for being too busy, and then the pandemic hit. This changed how I could run the business, so I made the decision to move into a proper industrial baking unit, hire staff and venture into postal bakes, all the while hosting bake-alongs on Instagram.

Over the last couple of years, I have thoroughly enjoyed creating fun videos on TikTok, Facebook and Instagram, and connecting with all of you lovely lot. I can't thank you all enough for the support over the years, even when I've been insufferable. If every social media 'like' was a £1 coin in my bum bag, I could retire in the Virgin Islands, with a nice little cottage on the south coast, a stately home and a butler but, alas, the struggle is real so please keep up the good work.

A lot of the bakes in this book are concepts I've come up with myself and made in many different variations over the years. You'll find fun, rebellious twists on classic treats like the Maple Syrup + Bacon Cake on page 190 and a whole host of my much-loved signature bakes like the Salted Caramel Cornflake Crevice on page 95 – this book is packed full of fun and interesting flavour combinations to help you get experimenting. There's so much fun to be had in adapting the recipes, and if you're inspired to create your own show-stopping variations, that would truly be the best form of flattery. There are recipes in the Back To Basics chapter, plus tips throughout the book, to help you add your own twists to the bakes. You'll find easy-to-follow, step-by-step instructions for each recipe which will guide you smoothly through the process. I love devising exciting platters brimming with different bakes and treats, so I hope you'll find this book packed with recipes that speak to you, and inspire you to go wild with baking up mouth-watering treats for friends and family.

Right, I could chunter on to you until the cows come home but to get to the point – happy baking!

George x

01

BEFORE YOU GET STARTED

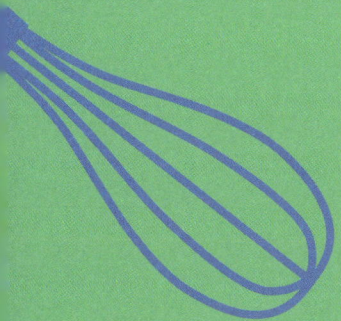

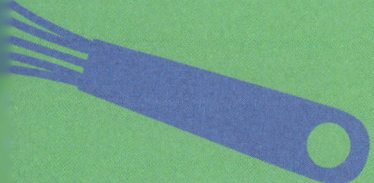

ESSENTIAL TOOLS

I have a confession. I typically *never* read the basics section at the front of cookbooks but OMG am I wrong – please make sure you read all of the information here, the whole recipes *and* the tips before even lifting a spatula!

These are my top tips for the best kit that will make your baking experience as easy as possible (and help you decipher what I'm talking about in some of the recipes). Finding the perfect tins, spoon spatulas and palette knives will massively help you along the way.

CAKE TINS

I like to keep it incredibly simple with the cake tins I use – typically, I use the round or square 20cm (8in) tins that are available to buy in most supermarkets or kitchenware stores. You can get them nice and cheap, but just make sure you hand wash them to retain their coating and they'll last you a long time. Where possible, I always recommend a loose-bottomed tins as you can get your bakes out of them so much more easily than from a fixed-base tin. If you can get your hands on them, my favourite tins are made by Masterclass – they're nice and deep (at least 7cm/2¾in), which is important as some of these bakes are really tall.

Where possible, avoid using a spring-form tin! They tend to leave an unpleasant rim around the base of whatever has been in them, and I can only assume they'll be used as belts for robots in the near future. Also try to avoid silicone bakeware – you will find the edges of cakes will form less of a crust, which is important to keep the structure of bakes. Silicone is more useful for moulds to set layers, as you'll see in some of the tart recipes in this book.

KITCHEN SCALES

For the best accuracy, make sure you weigh out all of your ingredients with a set of scales – I use the metric system throughout. Also, let it be known for anything measured in millilitres in this book, I don't trust my eyesight or the lines on a jug to measure fluids out. My vision is so bad that half the time I can't tell a cockapoo from a cockatoo! Just use the millilitre setting on your scales or, alternatively, just measure in grams – the amounts are the same.

For those of you who prefer to bake using the (very grand sounding) imperial system, the conversions are included throughout and there's also a conversion table on page 204. For consistency, just make sure you use either the metric *or* the imperial measurements within each recipe – don't mix and match them.

MEASURING SPOONS

Lots of recipes list ingredient quantities in tsp (teaspoon/5g) or tbsp (tablespoon/15g). If you don't have access to these, feel free to measure using your scales.

ELECTRIC STAND MIXER

I use a stand mixer to make everything – literally everything! If you're serious about your home baking, then I highly recommend investing in one. However, you can get great results with a hand-held electric whisk or, if you're up for the challenge, a wooden spoon and mixing bowl can even do the trick. It's best to use a paddle attachment for buttercreams and batters, and whisks for anything involving sugar syrups, meringues, and aerating eggs.

MIXING BOWLS

Mixing bowls are an essential bit of kit so you'll definitely need a couple of them at your disposal. I'm obsessed with the ones that have grips on their base for extra sturdiness. If you're using one without grips, place a tea towel beneath your bowl to stop it doing the cha-cha slide all over your countertop. Any time you work with egg whites, for instance when making meringues, always use a clean, dry bowl (preferably stainless steel or glass) so that no fat or grease mixes with the whites. Fat stops the protein in the egg whites forming solid bubbles and prevents them from whipping to their fullest, stiffest potential.

Also, avoid pouring large quantities of sugar syrup into small mixing bowls if using a hand whisk (e.g. when making nougat or marshmallows), as the mixture can splatter everywhere and you may easily burn yourself!

BAIN-MARIE

A bain-marie is simply a pan filled with barely simmering water over a low heat. Place a mixing bowl over it to melt ingredients together. Ideally, use a glass bowl. Metal will work, but conducts heat very quickly, meaning you might burn your fingers trying to move it on and off the heat, so take care. Don't use plastic bowls – they can melt! You also wanna make sure that every now and again, you lift your bowl up if your pan doesn't have pouring points to allow steam to escape. Remember – steam can burn!

SPATULAS

I detest food waste. I wanna get every last drop outta that mixing bowl, and the best thing I can recommend for this is a silicone spoon spatula. They're affordable, ridiculously easy to clean and super durable. They're also great for getting everything off the bottom of your pans.

SIEVE

A standard handheld sieve is all you need to pretend you're playing the tambourine while knocking lumps out of your mixture. Make sure you don't use a sieve larger than your mixing bowl otherwise you'll have particles everywhere.

THERMOMETERS

Sugar thermometer: To accurately measure sugar syrups for meringues and nougat, and to make sure some bakes are cooked just right, a sugar thermometer is essential. Instead of solid ones like a ruler, aim for digital meat thermometers that fold up and give a faster, more accurate reading.

Oven thermometer: At the bakery, we use a fan-assisted oven at all times – it controls the heat regularly, evenly and the temperature's always gonna be slightly lower than that required for a non-fan-assisted oven. All ovens cook slightly differently though, so I recommend using an oven thermometer for ultimate accuracy. You may find that you need to increase your temperature by 10°C (18°F) or a maximum of 20°C (36°F), so do take the baking times with a pinch of salt and adjust as required.

COOLING RACK

A wire rack is ideal to help bakes cool faster, or you can use trivets that are raised from the countertop.

TURNTABLE

When it comes to icing cakes, I do not care to spend hour upon hour trying to make them look as perfect as can be and much prefer a rustic look. I tend to ice my cakes on pieces of parchment paper and use a turntable to help smooth around the edges (the lazy-susan style spinning action makes it easy to evenly scrape the sides). They're great for avoiding any awkward angles when smoothing buttercreams or toppings on your cake.

CAKE BOARD

A cake board is a sturdy foil disc or square that the cake sits on for presentation, support or transportation purposes. If you want to ice your cake on a cake board, use one that's 2in (5cm) bigger than the tin size you used for your cake. This leaves a 1in (2.5cm) perimeter of board around the entire cake that allows you to carry it easily. Use a little buttercream or meringue to anchor the cake to the board. Alternatively, ice it on a plate or cake stand.

PALETTE KNIFE

A small palette knife with an angled blade is something I take most places with me – it's handy for far more than just icing cakes, such as smoothing over and levelling out toppings or caramel.

SERRATED KNIFE

Level your cake layers with a serrated knife as much as possible when you're planning to stack them. This ensures your cake has a fairly flat, level top. Wire cake levellers are also great for this.

CAKE SCRAPER

To get a smooth finish on your iced cakes, you'll need a cake scraper which is a simple, nifty tool with a straight edge that you glide around the outside of your iced cake for an even surface. That said, I find a dough cutter more efficient – it's got a nice grip and is more likely to be at least the height of the cake. Running the metal under hot water before scraping the cake makes the finish much smoother.

METAL SKEWER

This is a great tool for testing the readiness of your bakes – sponge cakes in particular. If it comes out clean, your cake is ready.

PIPING BAGS AND NOZZLES

Buying a large roll of piping bags often works out cheaper, and lots of them are reusable (if you can be bothered to wash them!). They're incredibly handy for filling cookie sandwiches and wagon wheels, decorating and even stacking cakes – pipe the buttercream evenly across the sponge, rather than spreading it and shifting the layers. You don't even need to use a nozzle – simply snip away the end of the bag – but any basic nozzle set will be versatile enough for any style or technique.

PARCHMENT PAPER

Make sure it's non-stick and greaseproof (why do they create anything else?) and beware of the some more expensive brands as they can end up sticking to your bakes. Supermarket own brands are probably going to serve you best.

CLING FILM

Another kitchen essential at the bakery! Cling film is great for keeping your bakes fresh and moist when you need to leave them to sit before moving on to the next stage. It's also a great tool if you're worried about your cake collapsing while you're icing it – wrap that thing in cling film like someone has had a facelift and chuck it in the fridge. Leave it to chill for at least half an hour to firm up, then you can assess the damage.

BAKING BEANS

Used with parchment paper, these little ceramic balls stop your tart pastry from puffing up and losing its shape in the oven.

INGREDIENTS

To make all of these bakes exactly as I do, take into account my top tips for ingredients which will really make the difference in the overall quality and end result of your bakes.

BUTTER

Unless stated otherwise, I'll always be using softened, unsalted butter in my recipes. Where possible, avoid using baking block or margarine – it just ain't the one and will affect the taste and texture of your bakes. For all of the cake recipes, you're gonna wanna leave that butter out at room temperature (unless otherwise stated) to soften for the best results.

EGGS

It's gotta be large and, at the very least, free range – so don't be using eggs from a caged clucker! Large eggs weigh around 60g (2¼oz) – comprised of roughly 40g (1½oz) of egg white and 20g (¾oz) of yolk – so if you only have medium eggs to hand, you can use this as a rough measurement to guide you.

SUGAR

Caster sugar: This is the most common sugar used throughout the book – I even use it instead of granulated sugar to make syrups as it dissolves much more quickly. As someone who doesn't see the pleasure in pouring scalding drinks down my oesophagus, I never have granulated in the house!

Brown sugars: These are less refined so contain molasses, which means that if you don't have any in, you can add black treacle to your caster sugar for the same results.

FLOUR

I'm a fan of self-raising flour for most of my cakes. If you only have plain flour in the cupboard, you can make your own self-raising flour by adding a teaspoon of baking powder for every 100g (3½oz) of plain flour (though this might get costly!). You can also make lots of the cakes gluten free by simply swapping the flour for gluten-free flour and adding two tablespoons of moisture (whether it be a form of flavouring such as lemon juice, alcohol or vanilla, or just milk).

CHOCOLATE

Use the best quality chocolate you can find or even just your favourite brand – it really will make your bakes taste much nicer.

SALT

Whenever I call for salt in my recipes, I am talking salt flakes. I have changed people's lives by introducing them to Maldon sea salt flakes. You are gonna wanna sprinkle them on every single thing you put in your mouth. I have a very sweet tooth so feel free to turn down the sweetness in any recipe slightly by adding a little sprinkling of salt. I'm talking in cheesecake bases, on the top of a rocky road or sprinkled on a cookie. Go wild.

FOOD COLOURING

The best you can get is Colour Mill oil-based food colouring. They have hundreds of different shades and you can even use a whitener to transform buttercream into a blank, snowy canvas before you start adding colour. These colourings are more expensive than your traditional supermarket food colouring, but the pigment is much stronger and will last you a lot longer, so it's worth the investment. If you can't get your hands on Colour Mill, I recommend always opting for another oil-based food colouring where you can.

Lotus

VANILLA AND OTHER FLAVOURINGS

I'm a vanilla elitist so, for me, only vanilla bean paste will do! The best substitute for it, however, is vanilla bean extract. The only type of vanilla I would steer clear of is vanilla essence. It's much cheaper, but is synthetic and won't taste anywhere near as good as the real thing.

DAIRY

I only use whole milk in bakes, and the cream used is always double cream unless stated otherwise.

BRANDED CONFECTIONARY

I use lots of popular branded chocolate and other sweet treats in my bakes. If you can't find an exact match, you can get creative with alternatives! The recipes always tell you the weight of the chocolate needed to help you get a great match.

JAMS, JELLIES AND CONSERVES

While super simple to make yourself, there's no harm in buying these – try to choose a a good quality (or high end) conserve which will be less sweet. It's best to muddle it (use a spoon to mash it in the jar) to help loosen the consistency and make it easier to spread.

GETTING PREPPED

When getting started on any recipe, a bit of careful preparation will make things so much easier and a lot less stressful (especially if you are baking with children!). Here are a few tips to get the most from your preparations:

- Familiarize yourself with the recipe. Read through all the ingredients and the method carefully – this way you know exactly the ingredients and equipment you'll need.
- Make ample space on your countertop – even the simplest recipe is even easier when you have space to work.
- Weigh out all your ingredients (see page 10).
- If required, preheat your oven to the stated temperature.
- Line your tin(s) – see below for guidance.

LINING TINS

The ease of lining a tin depends on its shape and size. I always prefer to use a deep tin, so more parchment paper is gonna be required, and to prevent it from falling into your bakes you're gonna need to secure it properly. The best tool I have found for this is cheap margarine/spread. While I don't condone using anything other than butter in the recipes (I repeat – no baking block!) using spread to help line the tins is the easiest way to keep your parchment paper anchored. To do this, use a piece of kitchen roll to scoop up a little bit and smear all over your tins, all the way to the very top. Then push in and stick down a pre-cut sheet of parchment paper.

To line a square tin:

1. Cut a piece of parchment paper that's larger than your tin by roughly 10cm (4in) either side (assuming your tin is roughly 8cm/3in deep).
2. Use your hands to gently push the sheet into the corners of the tin, then remove and set aside – this will make it easier to slot in once you've greased the tin.
3. Grease the tin (sides and base) and push the paper back into the tin. Secure the base first, making sure there are no wrinkles or grooves in the paper.
4. Fold the corners of the paper, ensuring it's flat against the edges – with any extra paper flopping to the side of the corners. Make an incision down the paper against one corner and fold the paper so it hangs against the adjacent side. Slice this and any excess off while leaving a slight cover so no mixture ends up stuck to the tin. Repeat for the other three corners.

To line a round tin:

5. Grease the sides and base of the tin.
6. Remove the base of the tin, lay it on your roll of parchment paper and draw around the edge (position the base against the edge of the roll so that you don't waste any paper), then cut out.
7. Line the base and return it to the tin.
8. Cut strips of paper 2.5cm (1in) higher than the sides of the tin, and wrap around the inside edges. (You might have a handy rectangle of paper left next to the circular hole for this.)

GEORGE'S BIG TIPS

Keep it clean
Wrap the top of your stand mixer in cling film – it's gonna stop mixture spurting, splattering and clouding the surrounding area. Most stand mixers come with guards but they're about as useful as a chocolate teapot – icing sugar still comes out like a volcanic explosion and covers the entire kitchen! You can also use a tea towel, but something disposable means no chance of cross-contamination.

In case of an emergency…
My Capricorn-ness means I'm overly pessimistic, stressed and hugely critical, all of which has added to the fear that I could pass away at any minute and people at my wake would be moaning about how bad the food is… If that was the case, I couldn't live with myself! So, I always make sure I have a chest freezer full of cakes and bakes (both iced and uniced) that I replace once a year in case of my own death. What this means is that I know just how well most of these bakes freeze! Just make sure you wrap up everything to the extent that any freezer-raiders will think you're into mummification. Put the cakes in the fridge to thaw before eating so as not to leave them in a textural mush.

CHILL OUT

Before you start any baking, make sure you have space in your fridge – so many of our recipes require refrigeration. I have mine set to 2°C (36°F) to make bakes cool faster. Just make sure you don't put any hot cake tins onto the shelves in your fridge! Rapid heating or cooling of glass causes it to smash and crack, so leave your tins to cool on the side for at least 15 minutes before putting them in the fridge. When you do put your cakes and bakes in the fridge, make sure you're laying them flat. If leaving something to set for hours or overnight, make sure everything in your fridge is covered – no one wants to eat a cheesecake that's taken on the flavour of your leftover teriyaki salmon!

WHAT'S IN STORE?

All of the cakes and bakes are best stored in the fridge. Keep them in airtight containers or tightly wrapped in cling film to prolong their shelf life as best as possible.

LIKE A KNIFE THROUGH BUTTER(CREAM)

Getting the perfect slices of traybakes and cakes can be a lot more difficult than you'd think, so here are my top tips:

- Use a long, strong knife that's bigger than your tin and can cut through your bake in one go. My favourite is a ginormous Victorinox 30.5cm (12in) knife that is bigger than any tin I use.
- Run the knife under hot water for a minute before slicing. It will melt as it cuts, meaning that your layers stay defined after slicing.
- Clean and re-heat the knife between every incision.
- Leave traybakes out of the fridge for about 30 minutes before slicing. If too cold, they can crumble upon cutting.

02

BACK TO BASICS

After plain cakes, brownies and cookies, I consider these recipes to be among the most vital in your repertoire, serving as the building blocks to raise your baking game, adding new layers and textures that elevate your creations. Whenever I'm stuck for new ideas at the bakery, I always come back to these essentials.

Both of the caramels in this chapter are best left to cool before you use them – pouring them while still warm can cause your bakes to melt, destroying all those well-defined layers. Thiccc Caramel (see page 26) in particular will continue to gain thicccness as it cools and can be used like a spread. Salted Caramel (see page 28) can be drizzled over pretty much anything to make it better.

Ganache is perfect for sandwiching cookies, as layers in cakes, used as drips and to fill cookie cups. You can even swirl different types of ganache together on a serving platter to create a ganache board – just grab your favourite slices and scoop!

Nougat has also become a staple component of creations at the bakery. It might seem hard to make, but it's so simple (imagine the Italian meringue with added whisking and ingredients in the syrup). The resulting fluffy, pillowy delicacy can honestly be smothered on any bake (so far we've added it to salted caramel cornflakes, blondies, brownies and rocky roads, and it pairs perfectly with every single one!).

The Edible Cookie Dough recipe (see page 34) in this chapter is another quick-to-rustle-up treat that can be enjoyed in its own right. Eat it out of a bowl or smother and drizzle it with caramel to make it an easy dessert when you want some speedy indulgence.

Like me, you'll find lots of opportunities to add to any of these modest recipes. Mixed and matched with the cakes, cookies, slices and brownies in this book, you'll soon be creating bakes even greater than the sum of their parts.

THICCC CARAMEL

I am obsessed with thiccc caramel – yes, that's right, three Cs. I would happily spread this over a chocolate bar in the morning and call it breakfast instead of your boring old toast and butter. It can be used in so many bakes and, lemme tell ya, real love is making this, jarring it up and giving it out as gifts!

At the bakery, we make roughly twenty-five times this amount in our caramel machine, which takes around seven hours. Before that, we made seven times this at once in large stock pots. It was pretty much someone's full-time job and they could've given The Rock a run for his money in the guns department with all the stirring. This recipe makes the perfect quantity to get you started!

Prep time: 20 minutes
Makes: 1kg (2lb 3oz)

175g (6oz) butter
115g (4oz) light brown sugar
115g (4oz) golden syrup
750g (1lb 10oz) condensed milk

1. Put all your ingredients in a saucepan and start by stirring infrequently over a low heat with a spatula. Make sure to catch and break down any harder lumps of sugar while it dissolves and the butter is melting.

2. Once the butter and the sugar has dissolved, and the butter is combined into the mixture, turn the heat up to medium-high.

3. Begin stirring continuously for 25–35 minutes (make sure the caramel doesn't catch on the bottom) until it begins to darken in colour. If you have a thermometer to hand, look for a temperature between 93–103°C (199–217°F). Another way to test if you're on the right track is by scooping up a teaspoon of the caramel and dropping a small amount into a glass of cold water. If a ball forms, your caramel is ready.

4. Take it off the heat, but continue whisking for a couple of minutes to ensure that the residual heat in the pan doesn't burn or catch the caramel on the bottom.

GEORGE LOVES A TIP!

— Fancy switching up the flavour? Drop in 200g (7oz) of your favourite spread into the warm caramel. My go-to is Nutella for a hazelnutty-gooey fusion.

SALTED CARAMEL

This salted caramel is the base for a huge amount of my products and it's incredibly easy to make it yourself at home. The first time I tried this recipe was in my mum's little kitchen. I was so scared it would splatter everywhere and I'd burn myself that I wore oven gloves the entire time and had sand buckets and a fire extinguisher ready to go! But then, I have always been a drama queen.

For making your salted caramel at home, a deep saucepan with a heavy bottom is a must. I recommend one with a capacity of 3 litres (5¼ pints) – the caramel will never bubble higher than halfway up the pan, so you'll be completely safe!

Prep time: 30 minutes
Makes: 800g (1lb 12oz)

450g (1lb) granulated sugar
300g (10½oz) butter
250ml (8½fl oz) double cream
1½ tbsp salt flakes

1. Place the sugar in a deep, heavy-bottomed saucepan on a medium-high heat, without stirring, until the sugar starts to melt.
2. When the sugar begins to melt, gradually start stirring. Make sure to get any lumps of sugar from the edges of the pan back into the middle so that everything melts and begins to caramelize.
3. In a second saucepan, warm your double cream over a low heat until steaming. Don't let it get too hot or boil.
4. When the sugar has completely melted and started to turn an amber colour, start adding the butter over a low heat. Add this in slowly – just a couple of tablespoons at a time. Whisk in between additions (take care as the caramel will froth and rise up) until all of the butter is incorporated.
5. Slowly pour in the warmed cream and whisk gently to combine until all incorporated. Add the salt flakes, stirring them through the mixture, then remove your salted caramel from the heat.

CAKE DRIPS

Prep time: 5 minutes
Makes: Enough for 2 x 20cm (8in) cakes

We decorate the majority of our cakes with drips. It's a really versatile way of adding colour, as well as helping to stick on any toppings! For most cakes, we use a chocolate drip, and for adding colour you need to start with white chocolate. Simply add your food colouring to the mixture to make it any shade you like. For optimal results, add a drop of white food colouring before any other shade to remove its creamy twang! There's also a recipe for a pistachio drip perfect for my Pistachio, White Chocolate + Raspberry Cake on page 158.

Dark Chocolate Drip:
100g (3½oz) dark chocolate
90g (3¼oz) soft butter

White Chocolate Ganache Drip:
100g (3½oz) white chocolate
75ml (2½fl oz) double cream, removed from the fridge 10 minutes before use

Pistachio Drip:
100g (3½oz) pistachios
40ml (1½fl oz) vegetable oil
1 tbsp caster sugar
100g (3½oz) white chocolate, melted

TO MAKE THE DARK CHOCOLATE DRIP:

Melt the dark chocolate in a microwave on a medium heat setting (around 500 watts) in 15-second intervals until completely melted. Dollop in the butter and mix until melted through. The mixture should be glossy.

TO MAKE THE WHITE CHOCOLATE DRIP:

Melt the white chocolate in a microwave on a medium setting in 15-second intervals until completely melted. Allow to cool for 1 minute before stirring in the double cream until glossy and smooth. You may have to wait for the ganache to cool to reach the desired consistency.

TO MAKE THE PISTACHIO DRIP:

1. Blitz the pistachios in a food processor until they break down. This can take five minutes or more, so keep scraping down the sides of the bowl and give the food processor a rest so it doesn't overheat!
2. When a paste starts to form, and with the blades running, pour in the oil bit by bit until the pistachio paste thins out a little. Add the caster sugar and blitz again.
3. Transfer the pistachio mix to a bowl and mix through the melted white chocolate before dripping it down your cake.

GEORGE LOVES A TIP!

— Pour your drip onto the centre of the chilled cake and use a palette knife to gently move the drips to the edges of the cake, allowing it to drip down the sides. It will set as it cascades.

— Alternatively, fill a piping bag with the mixture to better control the drips down the rim of the cake, before filling in the middle. To vary the lengths of the drips, apply varied amounts of pressure to the bag to create each droplet.

— Always add the drip to a chilled cake, this will allow it to set as it flows downward.

— If your drip isn't dripping, or is setting faster than you'd like, ensure your cake is secure on its turntable, then spin it.

GANACHE

You'll see in the many delights this book has to offer, I use lots of ganache. As I primarily use it for construction purposes (or for when I'm in a hurry to get home and watch a season of *The Real Housewives*), I opt for an unconventional melting method. For the most part this means using a microwave to melt my chocolate before pouring and beating in the cream. Conventional ways of making ganache include either heating your cream in a saucepan, then pouring over finely chopped chocolate, or just melting chopped chocolate in a saucepan with your cream until it creates a gorgeous, glossy ganache. This is my standard recipe, plus a few how-tos for variations you may come across in the book.

Prep time: 5 minutes
Makes: 800g (1lb 12oz)

500g (1lb 2oz) milk chocolate
300ml (10fl oz) double cream, at room temperature

1. If starting with a bar of chocolate, break it up into equal-sized chunks and pop into a mixing bowl. Melt the chocolate in a microwave on a medium setting in 30-second intervals – stirring between each – until completely melted.
2. Place the bowl on a tea towel and use a spatula to slowly beat the mixture as you gradually pour in the cream to form a ganache. You're basically whipping it (without a whisk!) to form part way between a whipped texture and a flowing, silky texture.

WHITE CHOCOLATE GANACHE:

White chocolate has a much higher percentage of cocoa butter than milk or dark chocolate, so will result in a runnier ganache. To reduce the risk of the ganache splitting, allow the white chocolate to cool for a lot longer before adding cream that's just above fridge temperature.

DARK CHOCOLATE GANACHE:

Dark chocolate sets a lot faster than milk or white chocolate, which makes it a really great option for constructing bakes! If mixed with cream straight from the fridge, it would create an incredible, structurally-sound ganache for use in recipes such as Cookie Sandwiches (see page 115).

GEORGE LOVES A TIP!

— Why not make a ganache charcuterie board? Dollop and smear a mix of milk, white and dark chocolate ganache over a wooden board. Use slices of fresh fruit and/or bakes such as brownies (see page 48) and cookies (see pages 119 and 122) to scoop up the ganache and enjoy!

— For thick ganache that's ready to pipe, use double cream straight from the fridge.

EDIBLE COOKIE DOUGH

Prep time:
5 minutes, plus chilling
Makes: 750g (1lb 10oz)

Regular cookie dough isn't edible due to its raw eggs and flour which can impact on your insides like something out of a Ridley Scott film. Edible cookie dough, however, ain't gonna kill ya! Also, let it be known that edible cookie dough is going to be slightly grainy, and that's because the sugar isn't cooked or fully dissolved. The longer you beat and cream the mixture, the softer it'll be.

250g (9oz) plain flour
225g (8oz) softened butter
200g (7oz) light brown sugar
100g (3½oz) chocolate, chips or chopped
Pinch of salt, optional

1. Preheat your oven to 180°C/160°C fan/350°F/Gas 4.
2. Spread out your flour on a baking tray and bake in the oven for 8 minutes. Leave to cool until it's just warm to the touch*.
3. Beat your sugar and butter on a medium speed to start, before gradually increasing to high speed until your mixture is light, fluffy and creamalicious.
4. Sieve in the heat-treated plain flour and mix some more until a soft cookie dough forms. If needed, you can add a couple of tablespoons of milk to thin out the mixture, vanilla or salt to flavour it, and any kind of chocolate you want to make it tasty.

GEORGE LOVES A TIP!

— This is great for decorating cakes and sweet treats – we scoop this to top our cookie cups (see page 105) and on the Cookies, Cream + Everything In-Between Cake (see page 192).

— Warm up in the microwave in bursts for a gooey dessert, but make sure not to heat it too long or you'll have a gunky mess.

— *My sister once tried to cool the flour by placing it near an open window (much to the amusement of Hetty the hoover, who was snorting flour from the floor for several minutes afterwards), so don't do this.

ITALIAN MERINGUE

Most people seem to panic when they hear about Italian meringue, but it's incredibly easy to make and is a great way to make a dessert even naughtier! It differs from regular meringue as it involves syrup, timings and maybe a little panic – it's also Italian and therefore hotter. You can pipe it onto brownies and toast it, stack cakes with it, top pies and tarts with it, spread it over cookies and stick them together, and even just eat it straight!

Prep time: 15 minutes
Makes: Enough to stack and coat a 2-layer, 20cm (8in) cake

---

6 egg whites (240g 8½ oz)
½ tsp cream of tartar
200ml (6¾fl oz) water
300g (10½oz) caster sugar

1. Place the egg whites and cream of tartar in a mixing bowl. Meanwhile, place the water and sugar in a saucepan on a medium heat until the sugar has dissolved before turning it up to a high heat and boiling to create a sugar syrup.

2. When the syrup reaches 112°C (233°F), begin whisking the egg whites on a low speed. When the syrup reaches 116°C (240°F), whisk the eggs on a medium speed. When the syrup reaches 120°C (248°F), remove the saucepan from the heat, whisk the egg whites on high speed, and slowly pour the syrup into the egg whites as they whisk. Once all of the syrup has been poured into the meringue mixture, gradually reduce the speed of the whisk to help keep the meringue stable and allow it to cool down.

3. You can either dollop the meringue on top of your bakes, or use a piping bag with your favourite nozzle to decorate. This meringue can also be eaten as it is or even blowtorched/grilled to char and add more flavour.

GEORGE LOVES A TIP!

— The meringue is most malleable when still slightly warm.

— The heat of the syrup cooks the egg whites, so the meringue is safe to eat without toasting.

— You can add food colouring or flavouring to mix up the meringue – a little will go a very long way.

NOUGAT

Prep time: 25 mins
Makes: Enough to cover an 8in (20cm) tin.

This recipe is a long way away from that set stuff crammed full of nuts – this is a deliciously creamy nougat, perfect as a layer in one of your favourite bakes. It can be a little bland on its own, but sandwiched between chocolate and ganache it's like a creamier marshmallow fluff that helps bring everything together! There's a reason it's in so many famous chocolate bars...

250g (9oz) caster sugar
150g (5¼oz) honey
22g (¾oz) liquid glucose
125ml (4¼fl oz) water
2 egg whites (approx. 80g/3oz)

1. Start by placing the sugar, honey and liquid glucose in a heavy-bottomed saucepan with 125ml (4¼fl oz) of water. Warm over a medium heat until the sugar has dissolved and you have a syrup. Turn up the heat to high and start to boil the syrup – you want it to eventually reach 160°C (320°F) on a thermometer.

2. When the syrup reaches 145°C (293°F), whisk the egg whites to form soft peaks. When the syrup reaches 160°C (320°F), slowly trickle it into the egg whites while they whisk – be careful! The mixture will rise up and some of the syrup may spit out of the mixing bowl. Keep the mixer whisking on high speed for a couple of minutes before gradually slowing it down. The resulting nougat should now be thickening and sticking to the whisk attachment. By the time the mixture's ready, the bowl should be just warm to touch – this will take 3–5 minutes.

3. When thick and still slightly warm, pipe or spread the nougat however your heart desires!

GEORGE LOVES A TIP!

— Use a deep saucepan to make the syrup – it will bubble up ferociously as it reaches its maximum temperature.

— Use an oven glove to hold the syrupy saucepan as you pour it into the egg whites.

— Cleaning your pans and bowls after making this recipe can be a nightmare. The easiest way is to leave them to soak in very hot water to properly dissolve the sugar. Once it's all dissolved, drain and wash thoroughly.

SUPER SIMPLE PASTRY

Prep time: 20 mins
Makes: Enough for 6 x 4in (10cm) tart tins or 1 x 9" (23cm) tart tin

Pastry only takes a few minutes to make and can quickly be turned into the base of a dessert (just slap some ganache in there and throw a berry or two on top) – and it tastes so much nicer than the shop-bought stuff.

200g (7oz) plain flour
30g (1⅛oz) ground almonds
40g (1½oz) icing sugar
125g (4½oz) cold butter, cubed
1 large egg yolk
1 tbsp cold water

1. Pulse the flour, ground almonds and icing sugar in a food processor until incorporated.
2. Add the butter and egg yolk and pulse until combined, trickling the water in to help form a dough, if required.
3. Tip onto a work surface and bring together before rolling out and lining your tart tin(s). Refrigerate for 30 minutes.

Prep time: 20 mins
Makes: Enough for 6 x 4in (10cm) tart tins or 1 x 9" (23cm) tart tin

CHOCOLATE PASTRY

150g (5¼oz) plain flour
50g (2oz) cocoa powder
15g (½oz) ground almonds
30g (1⅛oz) icing sugar
125g (4½oz) cold butter, cubed
1 egg yolk
2 tbsp cold water

1. In a food processor, blitz together the flour, cocoa powder, ground almonds and icing sugar until combined.
2. Add the butter cubes and egg yolk and pulse until a dough starts to form. Slowly add the cold water to help the dough along.
3. Tip onto a work surface and bring together with your hands. Cover and chill in the fridge for 20 minutes. Roll the pastry out and line your tart tin(s). Refrigerate again for 20 minutes.

TO COOK THE PASTRY CASES:

1. Preheat your oven to 210°C/190°C fan/410°F/Gas 6.
2. Line your tin(s) with pastry, then add parchment paper and fill with baking beans.
3. Blind bake for 18 minutes before removing from the oven, taking out the beans and parchment and cooking for another 5 minutes. Leave to cool.

FRENCH MERINGUE BUTTERCREAM

Prep time: 25 mins
Makes: 550g (1lb 3oz) or enough to cover a 8in (20cm) cake

For me, the smoothest and most indulgent buttercream is French meringue buttercream, made with butter and egg yolks. The only con is that it's far less heat resistant and structurally sound than standard buttercream, so is best used for coating cakes or for use in the winter months.

150g (5¼oz) caster sugar
75ml (2½fl oz) water
8 egg yolks
250g (9oz) butter
1 tsp vanilla bean paste

1. Place the caster sugar and water into a saucepan and heat, without stirring, until the syrup reaches 116°C (240°F).
2. Meanwhile, place the egg yolks in a mixing bowl and whisk on high until they're pale and increase in volume. When the syrup reaches 116°C (240°F), slowly pour it into the egg yolks while whisking.
3. When all of the syrup has been incorporated, continue whisking on a medium speed for five minutes until the mixing bowl is cool to the touch.
4. You can now begin adding the butter, a tablespoon at a time. Wait for each spoonful to become incorporated before adding the next.
5. When all of the butter has been added, add in the vanilla and continue whisking until fully mixed.

GEORGE LOVES A TIP!

— For a super-simple buttercream, mix 300g (10½oz) of soft butter with 600g (1lb 5oz) icing sugar. Beat until light, fluffy and fully incorporated. This is also slightly less melty than French meringue buttercream.

— Fancy mixing this up? Add a flavouring of your choice.

— If your buttercream is too soft, you've just added butter that's too warm or the mixture has become too warm. Refrigerate, checking and stirring often, until your desired consistency is achieved.

03

TIN IT TO WIN IT

When I first knew I was going to be writing a cookbook, it was this chapter and a few of the recipes in it that instantly sprang to my mind. Bulges and brownies are some of the most popular bakes on our stall, and there's something so incredibly satisfying and simple about making everything in one tin.

Take my serving sizes with a pinch of salt in this chapter – all of these recipes can be sliced and served up in however many portions you'd like, whether those are mini bite-size pieces or giant cubes of deliciousness. Another traybake benefit is that many of these recipes are also perfect to make with kids because they're so straightforward and super fun! And if you like the idea of minimal washing-up, the Best-Ever Caramel Flapjack (see page 54), Shortbread Smiles (page 55) and Ultimate Triple Chocolate Brownie (see page 48) are perfect for less clean-up time when you're finished.

When it comes to eating any of these bakes, don't be holding back now – the majority of these bakes are gonna leave you with sticky fingers and messy hands – and know that there's no shame in eating the entire tray in one sitting...

PORNSTAR MARTINI CHEESECAKE BLONDIES

Prep + baking time:
45 minutes, plus chilling
Serves: 12

I dabbled with the thought of baking a cheesecake into these blondies. But pornstar martinis are for summer, and so the refreshing and cooling mixture of cold, no-bake cheesecake smothered over this fruity blondie makes much more sense!

For the blondies:
200g (7oz) white chocolate
250g (9oz) butter
300g (10½oz) golden caster sugar
185g (6½oz) plain flour
15g (½oz) cornflour
1 tsp vanilla bean paste
4 eggs
100g (3½oz) white chocolate chips
75ml (2½fl oz) passion fruit coulis

For the cheesecake topping:
300g (10½oz) cream cheese
50g (2oz) icing sugar
150g (5¼oz) double cream
2 tbsp Passoa passion fruit liqueur
50ml (2fl oz) passion fruit coulis

1. Preheat your oven to 160°C/140°C fan/320°F/Gas 3. Grease and line a 20cm (8in) square cake tin.
2. To make the blondies, start by melting the chocolate and butter together in a bowl over a bain-marie, mixing to combine.
3. Add to the bowl the sugar, plain flour, cornflour, vanilla bean paste and eggs, and beat until smooth. Stir through the chocolate chips, then pour the batter into a tin. If needed, use a palette knife to spread it out into the corners.
4. Drizzle over the passion fruit coulis, then use a palette knife to swirl everything together. Bake for 40-45 minutes.
5. Remove from the oven and leave to cool at room temperature for 20 minutes. Then refrigerate for at least 4 hours to 'set' and create the perfect chewy blondie texture.
6. To make the cheesecake topping, whisk together the cream cheese, icing sugar and double cream until thick, then add the Passoa and whisk once more.
7. Remove the blondies from the fridge and use a palette knife to smother them with the cheesecake topping. Drizzle the coulis over and swirl through the topping. Slice up and serve!

GEORGE LOVES A TIP!

— Store these in the fridge and eat within two days.

— To make these even more magical, slice up the blondies into your preferred portion size, then use a piping bag and nozzle to pipe the cheesecake on to each one separately before finishing with the drizzle.

— If you want to make these even boozier, add vanilla vodka to the cheesecake mix.

ULTIMATE TRIPLE CHOCOLATE BROWNIE

Prep + baking time:
50 minutes
Serves: 12

A lockdown gamechanger for me was improving this brownie recipe by whisking the eggs and sugar together, and also finding the perfect temperature for these beauties to be cooked at. The higher the quality of the ingredients, the better they'll taste. Setting in the fridge is essential for that perfect fudgy texture.

200g (7oz) dark chocolate
250g (9oz) butter
300g (10½oz) golden caster sugar
4 eggs
80g (3oz) cocoa powder
65g (2½oz) plain flour
1 tsp salt
100g (3½oz) milk chocolate chips
100g (3½oz) white chocolate chips

1. Preheat your oven to 160°C/140°C fan/320°F/Gas 4. Grease and line a 25 x 20cm (10 x 7¾in) square cake tin.
2. Melt the chocolate and butter together in a bowl, over a bain-marie, mixing to combine.
3. In a mixing bowl, whisk the sugar and eggs together on a high speed for 3–5 minutes until pale, fluffy and at least double in size.
4. Gently pour the chocolate and butter mixture down the side of the mixing bowl and continue to whisk until combined.
5. Sieve the cocoa powder and plain flour into the liquid ingredients and gently fold in until lump-free. Add in the salt and chocolate chips and fold a couple more times, then pour the batter into the tin.
6. Bake for 22–26 minutes. The brownie is ready when it has a slight wobble and cracks on top, or when a thermometer reads 89°C (192°F). Leave to cool at room temperature for 30 minutes before setting in the fridge for at least 90 minutes.

GEORGE LOVES A TIP!

— If you only have an 20cm (8in) square cake tin to hand, you'll need to bake your batter for 45 minutes instead. Avoid overfilling your tin to allow enough space for your mixture to rise as it bakes.

STICKY UNDERCARRIAGE BLONDIES

Prep + baking time: 80 minutes
Serves: 12

Sticky, chewy-bottomed blondies add a little bit extra of texture to what are otherwise fairly smushy slabs of succulence. Use whichever sugar-shelled choc you can get your hands on – they seem to be very festive, so look out for a great selection at celebratory times of the year!

- 200g (9oz) white chocolate
- 250g (7oz) butter
- 300g (10½oz) caster sugar
- 275g (9¾oz) plain flour
- 15g (½oz) cornflour
- 1 tbsp golden syrup
- 4 eggs
- 1½ tsp vanilla bean paste
- ½ tsp salt flakes
- 100g (3½oz) sugar-shell chocolate
- 100g (3½oz) white chocolate chips (optional)
- 200g (7oz) chocolate and/or sugar-shell chocolate
- 75g (2¾oz) spread of your choice (optional)

1. Preheat your oven to 180°C/160°C fan/350°F/Gas 4.
2. Grease and line a 25 x 20cm (10 x 8in) square cake tin. Place in the oven for 10 minutes to heat.
3. In the meantime, melt the white chocolate and butter together in a bowl over a bain-marie, mixing to combine. Place the sugar, plain flour, salt and cornflour into a mixing bowl.
4. When the 10 minutes are up, take your heated cake tin out of the oven and pour in the tablespoon of golden syrup along with 100g (3½oz) of the sugar-shell chocolate. Return to the oven for 8 minutes while you make your batter.
5. Pour the melted butter and chocolate mix into the flour and sugar mix, and add the eggs and vanilla bean paste. Beat until a smooth batter is formed. If using white chocolate chips, add those now along with the remaining 200g (7oz) sugar-shell chocolates – mix until combined.
6. When the 8 minutes are up, take the hot cake tin out of the oven and carefully pour the batter over the melted syrup and chocolate. If you're using spread, melt and drizzle this over the batter and carefully swirl through.
7. Return the tray to the oven for 40-45 minutes, until the edges of the blondie are set and the middle still jiggles.
8. Leave the blondie to cool at room temperature for 20 minutes before refrigerating for at least 4 hours to help set.

GEORGE LOVES A TIP!

— In step 5, make sure your butter and chocolate are still hot when pouring into the dry ingredients to ensure that the sugars dissolve and the batter is smooth.

— The setting time in the fridge is what gives these blondies the perfect texture, so don't be tempted to skip it!

— Feel free to mix it up with your chocolate/sugar-shell chocolate. My favourite ones to use for this recipe are M&Ms, Smarties and Galaxy Minstels.

WHITE CHOCOLATE TOBLERLONE TOWER

Prep + baking time: 2 hours, plus chilling
Serves: 9

Among dainty bakes, these towers look incongruous and rich but, lemme tell you something, you'll be shocked at how speedily and easily you can scoff one of these moisterpieces up! The nougat is the perfect lubricant to help the brownie and ganache oesophagusly-glissade – you'll end up trying not to devour the tray in a day!

For the brownie base:
100g (3½oz) dark chocolate
125g (4½oz) butter
2 eggs
150g (5¼oz) golden caster sugar
40g (1½oz) cocoa powder
35g (1¼oz) plain flour
¼ tsp salt flakes

For the nougat:
1 batch of Nougat (for recipe, see page 38)

For the ganache topping and decoration:
720g (1lb 6oz) white Toblerone (I used 2 x 360g/12¾oz bars)
300ml (10fl oz) double cream

1. Preheat your oven to 180°C/160°C fan/350°F/Gas 4. Grease and line a deep 20cm (8in) square cake tin.
2. To make the brownie base, melt the chocolate and butter together in a bowl, over a bain-marie. In a mixer, whisk together the eggs and sugar until thick and frothy. Pour in the melted chocolate and butter mixture, and whisk to combine.
3. Sieve in the cocoa powder and flour and fold through. Add the salt and fold through again. Pour into the prepared tin and bake for 22 minutes until only a slight jiggle remains on top and a thermometer reaches 89°C (192°F). Leave to cool for 15 minutes at room temperature, then refrigerate for 1 hour.
4. Follwowing the method on page 38, make the nougat. When thick, scoop the nougat from the mixer and spread over the brownie. Leave to cool briefly.
5. Cut nine triangles from one Toblerone bar and set aside. Place the leftover Toblerone (approximately 500g/1lb 2oz) into a microwavable bowl and melt, before stirring in the cream to create a glossy ganache. Spread a layer over the nougat. Portion the Toblerone triangles over the top of the ganache.
6. Refrigerate for at least 4 hours before slicing into nine portions.

GEORGE LOVES A TIP!

— There are 11 triangles in a Toblerone bar, but make sure you slice off the extra chocolate on each side of the nine Toblerone triangles used for decoration. Add these offcuts to the rest of the chocolate for the ganache.

— Use a hot knife, wiping after each incision, to get clean cuts of these layers.

— Nougat doesn't survive too well when it gets hot, so make sure the bakes are stored in the fridge.

BEST-EVER CARAMEL FLAPJACK

Prep time + baking time: 45 minutes
Serves: 9

A simple and speedy job, you can whip up this mixture in no time, then cram in an episode of *Parks and Recreation* while it bakes – the dream! When ready to eat, these flapjacks should be chewy and caramelly, with crisp edges and minimal effort required.

For the flapjack:
225g (8oz) butter
275g (10oz) golden syrup
165g (5¾oz) light brown sugar
60g (2¼oz) caster sugar
450g (1lb) oats
80g (3oz) Rolos (or the caramel chocolate of your choice), frozen

To decorate:
300g (10½oz) milk chocolate, melted
80g (3oz) Rolos (or the caramel chocolate of your choice)
50g (2oz) salted caramel sauce

1. Preheat your oven to 180°C/160°C fan/350°F/Gas 4. Grease and line a 25 x 20cm (10 x 8in) square cake tin. Place the Rolos in the freezer to chill – the nicely chilled chocolate will stay intact and won't melt in the pan..

2. Melt the butter, golden syrup, light brown sugar and caster sugar in a saucepan over a medium heat until everything's dissolved. Tip in the oats and toss-galore until all are coated in the sensational, sugary syrup. Add the frozen Rolos and toss some more.

3. Pour into the baking tray, smush to level out and cook for 30 minutes until golden on top with a slight wobble (give the pan a shake to check). As soon as it's out of the oven, use a fish slice/flipper to push the flapjack mixture down and flatten it. Leave to cool for 1 hour before removing from the tin. Leave to cool completely.

4. To decorate, pour the melted chocolate over the top of the flapjack. Chop up the last of the Rolos and sprinkle the pieces all over, then drizzle over the salted caramel sauce and leave to set before slicing into nine portions.

GEORGE LOVES A TIP!

— You aren't gonna think the flapjacks are cooked by how puffed up and wobbly they look, but I promise they'll be ready.

SHORTBREAD SMILES

Prep + baking time: 45 minutes
Serves: 15

These are so cute! And it's really hard not to consume half a tray in a sitting, but they're perfect to bake with kids. Feeling grumpy? A bit angry? Don't want to move your facial muscles? Just create a sandwich with two smiley circles instead.

For the shortbread:
200g (7oz) butter
250g (9oz) plain flour
75g (2¾oz) caster sugar

For the filling:
100g (3½oz) butter
200g (7oz) icing sugar
¼ tsp vanilla bean paste
150g (5¼oz) jam of your choice

1. Preheat your oven to 140°C/120°C fan/275°F/Gas 1. Grease and line a baking tray.
2. Make the shortbread dough by rubbing the butter into the flour until it resembles coarse breadcrumbs, then stir in the caster sugar and knead to form a dough. Refrigerate for 15 minutes.
3. Flour the work surface and use a rolling pin to roll out the dough to a 5mm (¼in) thickness. Use a round cutter and a round, smiley-face cutter of the same diameter to cut circles out of the shortbread. Place on the lined baking tray.
4. Bake for 15–18 minutes, then leave to cool.
5. Make the buttercream by beating the butter and icing sugar together until smooth, then add the vanilla bean paste.
6. Pipe a round of buttercream around the edge of the plain circular shortbreads, and fill the centres with a spoonful of jam. Finish by sandwiching a smiley shortbread on top.

GEORGE LOVES A TIP!

— You can use any jam you like for this, but I love raspberry the most – with seeds! You can also make these with lemon curd or chocolate spread.

BLACK FOREST BAR

Prep + baking time: 4 hours
Serves: 10

This Black Forest Bar is fruity and fresh (a bit like me). The cherry filling layer is part jam, part fruit wind-up, and keeps its shape really well when sliced, so you don't have an oozing mess on your hands. Adding a boozy touch of kirsch into the ganache is (not quite literally) the cherry on top that takes these to ultimate black forestyness.

For the base:
150g (5¼oz) butter
80g (3oz) caster sugar
120g (4¼oz) light brown sugar
3 egg yolks
165g (5¾oz) plain flour
60g (2¼oz) cocoa powder
½ tsp baking powder
¼ tsp bicarbonate of soda
75g (2¾oz) sour cherries

For the cherry filling:
500g (1lb 2oz) cherries, pitted
1 tbsp lemon juice
1 tbsp honey
½ tbsp cornflour

For the ganache:
225g (8oz) dark chocolate
225g (8oz) milk chocolate
600ml (20fl oz) double cream
75ml (2½fl oz) icing sugar
1 tsp kirsch (optional)

For the cream topping:
250g (9oz) mascarpone
250ml (8½ fl oz) double cream
2 tbsp kirsch (optional)
1 tsp vanilla bean paste (optional)
10 cherries, to decorate

1. To make the filling, start by chopping the cherries to a coarse consistency. Place in a saucepan on a medium heat. Add the lemon juice, honey and cornflour to the pan. Cook for 1 hour, stirring occasionally until the mixture thickens and the cherries start to break down.

2. Meanwhile, make the base by beating together the butter and sugars before adding the rest of the ingredients and mixing to form a dough. Push into the base of the tin and freeze for 1 hour. Roughly 10 minutes before your dough comes out the freezer, preheat your oven to 120°C/100°C fan/250°F/Gas ½, and grease and line a deep 20cm (8in) square cake tin.

3. Remove the base from the freezer and pour over the cherry filling mixture. Bake in the oven for 1 hour until the cherry filling is sticky and dry to the touch. Leave to cool and set for 30 minutes.

4. To make the ganache, melt the dark and milk chocolate together in the microwave or over a bain-marie before slowly stirring in the double cream. Add the kirsch if using and keep stirring to incorporate. Sieve in the icing sugar and mix once more before spreading over the cooled cherry filling. Allow to set in the fridge for 4 hours.

5. Finally, to make the cream topping, place the mascarpone and cream into a mixing bowl and whisk until thick. Add the kirsch and/or vanilla and whisk until incorporated. Slice the bake into ten servings before piping on the creamy whipped mixture and finishing with cherries.

GEORGE LOVES A TIP!

— Use the best quality fresh cherries you can find to really give the cherry layer oomph. But if the worst comes to worst, tinned or frozen will work.

CHOCOLATE, HAZELNUT + CARAMEL CAKE CUBE

Prep + baking time:
1 hour, plus
overnight chilling
Serves: 16

These might look like quite heavy chunks of hazelnutty deliciousness, but they are incredibly light and fluffy. The whole cube practically dissolves in your mouth. The chilling time might seem tedious, but is a must to ensure the cubes don't crumble and dissolve upon dipping. If the number of tins required is a bit overwhelming, see the tip below for a less tin-tastic option.

For the sponge:
6 whole eggs
200g (7oz) ground almonds
250g (9oz) caster sugar
6 egg whites
120g (4¼oz) cocoa powder
50g (2oz) butter, melted

For the filling:
150g (5¼oz) Thiccc Caramel (see recipe, page 26)
200g (7oz) chocolate hazelnut spread

For the chocolate dunk:
400g (14oz) dark chocolate
600g (1lb 5oz) chocolate spread, melted
100g (3½oz) chopped roasted hazelnuts

1. Preheat your oven to 180°C/160°C fan/350°F/Gas 4. Grease and line six 20cm (8in) square cake tins.
2. To make the sponge, begin by whisking the whole eggs, ground almonds and 200g (7oz) of the caster sugar in a mixing bowl until the mixture thickens and trebles in size.
3. Whisk the egg whites until foaming, then slowly sprinkle in the remaining 50g (2oz) of caster sugar to form soft peaks. While whisking fold a third of the egg whites through the egg yolk mixture to thin it out a bit before adding the rest of the egg whites, sieving in the cocoa powder and pouring the butter against the side of the bowl so that you don't knock air out of the mixture. Gently fold together then, once combined, divide the mixture equally between the six lined cake tins and bake for 11 minutes.
4. When cooled, layer the cakes in a clean, 20cm (8in) square lined cake tin. Alternate fillings between each layer – start with a cake layer topped with the spread, followed by a cake layer topped with the caramel. Repeat until the final layer of cake is placed on top. Chill overnight.
5. Remove the cake from the fridge and slice into 16 equal-sized pieces. Freeze these for 1 hour while you make the chocolate dunk.
6. To make the chocolate dunk, melt the chocolate in the microwave, stirring at 15-second intervals. When melted, mix with the spread and stir in the chopped roasted hazelnuts.
7. Line a tray with parchment paper. Use two forks to lower each frozen cake cube into the warm, nutty chocolate mix, covering it completely before removing and placing on the baking tray. Repeat with all of the cake cubes before refrigerating for 1 hour.

GEORGE LOVES A TIP!

— This recipe requires a lot of tins but, fear not, I've got an alternative. Make half the quantity of batter and spread across a greased and lined grill pan to bake all at once. Assemble the layers in a lined loaf tin – slice your cake into loaf-tin sized strips and stack, alternating caramel and spread. Chill overnight, then slice before dunking as in the recipe!

KINDER COOKIES + CREAM BULGE

Prep + baking time:
2 hours, plus chilling
Serves: 12

Chewy, gooey baked cookie, creamy cookie dough, thiccc caramel and a luscious nutty topping all melt in your mouth with this one. OMG everyone is all about the nut butter these days but what about a nut bulge?!

For the cookie base:
150g (5¼oz) butter
80g (3oz) caster sugar
120g (4¼oz) light brown sugar
2 egg yolks
225g (8oz) plain flour
½ tsp baking powder
¼ tsp bicarbinate of soda
200g (7oz) Kinder Chocolate bars (approx. 16 small bars)

For the cookie dough:
850g (1lb 14oz) Thiccc Caramel (see recipe, page 26)
1 quantity of Edible Cookie Dough (see page 34)
200g (7oz) Kinder Chocolate bars
½ tsp vanilla bean paste

For the white chocolate hazelnut topping:
20g (¾oz) white chocolate, melted
400g (14oz) white chocolate hazelnut spread

To decorate:
200g (7oz) Kinder Chocolate bars

1. Preheat your oven to 180°C/160°C fan/350°F/Gas 4. Grease and line a 20cm (8in) square cake tin.
2. To make the cookie base, cream the butter and sugars together until creamy, then add the egg yolks, flour, baking powder and bicarbonate of soda, and mix to form a dough. Push into the tin, then break up and push the chocolate bars into the top of the dough (it's fine if they're peeping slightly over the surface). Bake for 16 minutes until golden on top. Leave to cool.
3. Place the flour for the cookie dough on a baking tray and bake for 8 minutes. Leave to cool.
4. Make the Thiccc Caramel (see page 26) ready for the cookie dough.
5. To make the cookie dough (see page 34) beat the butter, sugar and cooled flour together in a pan and mix until combined. Add in the chocolate bars and vanilla bean paste and continue to mix.
6. Flatten the cookie dough onto the cooled cookie. Pour over the slightly cooled caramel, then set aside.
7. To make the white chocolate hazelnut topping, pour the melted chocolate into the melted spread and stir to combine. Pour this mixture over the caramel layer.
8. Finish by decorating with chocolate bars before refrigerating for at least 2 hours before serving.

GEORGE LOVES A TIP!

— Taking the bake out of the fridge for 30 minutes before slicing, combined with hot knife, will ensure you leave perfect layers on every bulge.

CHOCOLATE BULGE

Prep + baking time: 1½ hours, plus chilling
Serves: 12

Triple chocolate thicccalicious, sexilicious gorgeousness describes this towering bulge. These are a staple at market (especially because you can easily substitute the plain flour for gluten-free plain flour to make them gluten free) even if we do have to up the choc quantities in the layers so they don't melt in the summer.

For the brownie:
125g (4½oz) butter
100g (3½oz) dark chocolate
150g (5¼oz) caster sugar
2 eggs
40g (1½oz) cocoa powder
30g (1⅛oz) plain flour
¼ tsp salt

For the chocolate caramel layer:
750g (1lb 10oz) Thiccc Caramel (see page 26)
100g (3½oz) milk chocolate spread, melted

For the dark, milk and white chocolate topping:
400g (14oz) milk chocolate spread
200g (7oz) dark chocolate, melted

400g (14oz) milk chocolate spread
200g (7oz) milk chocolate, melted

400g (14oz) white chocolate spread
200g (7oz) white chocolate

1. Preheat your oven to 180°C/160°C fan/350°F/Gas 4. Grease and line a 20cm (8in) square cake tin.
2. To make the brownie, melt the dark chocolate and butter together in a bowl over a bain-marie. Whisk the sugar and eggs until pale and doubled in size. Pour in the melted chocolate and butter and fold through before sieving in the cocoa powder and flour, adding the salt and folding once more. Pour into the tin, bake for 16–20 minutes until it reaches 89°C (192°F) and leave to cool.
3. To make the chocolate caramel layer, mix the Thiccc Caramel (see page 26) with the melted chocolate spread until smooth. Immediately pour onto the brownie base and allow to cool.
4. To make the chocolate layers, melt the chocolate spread in the saucepan, then add the melted dark chocolate. Combine and pour over the chocolate caramel layer and refrigerate until set (around 30 minutes). Repeat for the next two chocolate layers. When all of the layers have set, remove from the fridge and slice.

MARS BAR SLICE

I have absolutely zero shame in just telling you to stack all four of these recipes together because lemme tell you something, these are melt-in-your-mouth, clagtastic gorgeousness! You could easily slice these up into tiny finger portions to feed a crowd. This is a great bake to jazz up any leftovers knocking about in your fridge.

Prep + baking time: 2 hours, plus cooling
Serves: 15

For the whole bake, make each of the following:

1 quantity of Ultimate Triple Chocolate Brownie (see page 48)
½ quantity of Thiccc Caramel (see page 26)
1 quantity of Nougat (see page 38)
1 quantity of Milk Chocolate Ganache (see page 32)

1. Preheat your oven to 180°C/160°C fan/350°F/Gas 4. Grease and line a 20cm (8in) square cake tin.
2. Follow the method for the Ultimate Triple Chocolate Brownie (see page 48), without the chocolate chips.
3. Follow the method for the Thiccc Caramel (see page 26).
4. Make the Nougat (see page 38).
5. Whip up some milk chocolate ganache (see page 32).
6. Once the brownie cools, layer the caramel, nougat and ganache on top and leave to cool.
7. Bish, bash, bosh; George is your boss!

04

HOB JOBS

The recipes in this chapter are, by and large, some of my favourites. Not only are they my favourites because they are deliciousness, sexiliciousness, gorgeousness bakeonified, but also because they require minimal effort – mostly just bain-maries and saucepans on the hob to get the job done.

Chocolate and caramel are in abundance in these recipes, so some of them can be quite pricey to make. But I would not recommend going for cheaper ingredient options, otherwise the general taste and texture of your slices will be off due to the low percentage of cocoa butter and milk in the chocolate. That being said, despite being a brand snob, I believe there's no shame in using dupes for some of the different flavours in the rocky roads, for example. We can keep costs down a little – the cost of living crisis ain't gonna get ya.

With most of these bakes, the fridge is your best friend. I have mine set to 2°C (35°F) just to speed up the cooling and setting processes so I can eat my bakes as quickly as possible. Make sure you cover your bakes while they're in the fridge so as not to taint them with the smell of anything else in there.

For me, the highlight of this particular chapter is my signature Salted Caramel Cornflake Crevice (see page 95). It's a recipe that, and it doesn't know it yet, is gonna transcend space and time because it's that amazing. Videos of me making it, wriggling my digits in glistening caramellow cornflakes, have been seen by millions on the internet – and for good reason. Now you can make one of my all-time bestselling creations, as many have tried to online anyway, with a recipe straight from the George's mouth!

ROCKY ROAD MANIA

Prep + hob time: 45 minutes, plus chilling
Serves: 15

I love a good rocky road. They're fun. They're versatile. You can literally put whatever you want in them. And let's be honest, rocky roads are more of an assembly job, akin to a chocolate salad, rather than any real sort of culinary expertise. Whenever I'm feeling in a creative rut, I dress in disguise and make my way down to my local budget supermarket and spend an hour or so walking around the chocolate and biscuit aisles. I put anything I wanna eat in my basket until I can decide on a theme, which in this case appears to be *all* the chocolate caramel.

600g (1lb 5oz) milk chocolate
75g (2¾oz) butter
250g (9oz) chocolate caramel spread
150g (5¼oz) mini marshmallows
150g (5¼oz) Tunnock's caramel wafers, chopped
100g (3½oz) Rolos
75g (2¾oz) Munchies
100g (3½oz) caramel chocolate, broken into chunks

For the topping:
600g (1lb 5oz) chocolate caramel spread
200g (7oz) milk chocolate, melted

To decorate:
1 tbsp Biscoff spread, melted
100g (3½oz) Rolos

CHOCOLATE CARAMEL ROCKY ROAD

1. Grease and line a 20cm (8in) square tin.
2. Melt the chocolate and butter together in a bowl over a bain-marie, mixing to combine.
3. In the meantime, melt the chocolate caramel spread over a low heat.
4. In a large mixing bowl, combine the mini marshmallows, chopped caramel wafers, Rolos, Munchies and chunks of caramel chocolate, and toss together, like a chocolate salad, to create a 'rubble'.
5. When the chocolate and butter mix has melted, pour it into the saucepan with the melted spread and stir occasionally (off the heat) until combined. Pour this chocolate mixture over the rocky road rubble and toss until everything is fully coated. Transfer to the tin and refrigerate for 2 hours.
6. For the topping, gently melt the chocolate caramel spread in a saucepan until smooth before pouring in the melted chocolate. Stir until fully combined. Remove the rocky road from the fridge and pour over the chocolate mix. Move and tilt the tin to level out the topping.
7. To garnish, drizzle the melted Biscoff spread over the top and use a knife to swirl through the chocolate topping to form a pattern. Decorate with the Rolos (or the caramel chocolate of your pleasing).
8. Leave to refrigerate for 4 hours or overnight. Remove from the fridge 1 hour before slicing.

Recipe continues overleaf

WHITE CHOCOLATE ROCKY ROAD

600g (1lb 5oz) white chocolate
75g (2¾oz) butter
250g (9oz) white chocolate spread
160g (5½oz) white chocolate KitKat Chunky*
180g (5½oz) white chocolate Twix*
150g (5¼oz) mini marshmallows
100g (3½oz) shortbread
*or other white-chocolate based confectionary

For the topping:
600g (1lb 5oz) white chocolate spread
200g (7oz) white chocolate, melted

1. Grease and line a 20cm (8in) square cake tin.
2. Melt the white chocolate and butter in a bowl over a bain-marie, mixing to combine. In a saucepan, warm the white chocolate spread until the texture thins out a little and set aside.
3. Roughly chop up the KitKat Chunky bars and Twix bars, and place in a mixing bowl with the mini marshmallows. Crumble in the shortbread to complete the rocky road rubble.
4. Very gently combine the melted chocolate and butter with the warmed chocolate spread. Pour over the rocky road rubble and toss to combine. Plop into the tin and refrigerate for 2 hours.
5. When the 2 hours are up, make the topping. Melt the white chocolate spread in a saucepan before adding the melted white chocolate. Stir together and pour over the chilled rocky road mix. Return to the fridge for 4 hours to set. Remove from the fridge 1 hour before slicing.

COOKIES + CREAM ROCKY ROAD

600g (1lb 5oz) white chocolate
75g (2¾oz) butter
250g (9oz) white chocolate spread
300g (10½oz) Oreo original cookies
200g (7oz) chocolate chip cookies
150g (5¼oz) mini marshmallows

For the topping:
200g (7oz) white chocolate
600g (1lb 5oz) white chocolate spread
150g (5¼oz) Oreo original cookies

1. Grease and line a 20cm (8in) square tin.
2. Melt the white chocolate and butter in a bowl, over a bain-marie, mixing to combine. Melt the white chocolate spread in a saucepan over a low heat and set aside.
3. Tip all the cookies into a large mixing bowl and crumble to a very coarse rubble. Mix through the mini marshmallows.
4. Combine the white chocolate and butter mixture with the melted white chocolate spread. Pour the whole mixture over the rubble and toss to combine. Tip into the cake tin and refrigerate for 2 hours.
5. When the 2 hours are up, make the topping. Melt the white chocolate spread in a saucepan before adding the melted chocolate. Stir together and pour over the chilled rocky road mix. Decorate with the Oreo cookies and return to the fridge for 4 hours to set. Remove from the fridge 1 hour before slicing.

600g (1lb 5oz) dark chocolate
75g (2¾oz) butter
250g (9oz) milk chocolate spread
100g (3½oz) digestive biscuits, crumbled
200g (7oz) Aero Peppermint Bars, broken up
200g (7oz) Aero Peppermint Bubbles
150g (5¼oz) mini marshmallows
100g (3½oz) golden syrup
½ tsp peppermint extract

For the topping:
400g (14oz) milk chocolate spread
200g (7oz) dark chocolate, melted
20 mint thins (approx 200g/7oz)

MINT ROCKY ROAD

1. Grease and line a 20cm (8in) square cake tin.
2. Melt together the dark chocolate and butter in a bowl over a bain-marie. Melt the chocolate spread in a saucepan over a low heat and set aside.
3. Into a large mixing bowl, add the crumbled digestive biscuits, broken Aero bars, Aero Bubbles and mini marshmallows. Pour the melted chocolate, and butter into the chocolate spread and stir to combine. Add in the mint extract. Leave to cool for a couple of minutes, then pour the whole mixture over the rubble and toss to combine. Push into the cake tin and refrigerate for 1 hour.
4. When the hour is up, make the topping. Melt the chocolate spread in a saucepan before adding in the melted chocolate. Stir together and pour over the chilled rocky road mix. Decorate by placing mint thins across the top and return to the fridge for 4 hours to set. Remove from the fridge 1 hour before slicing.

GEORGE LOVES A TIP!

— If you're using aerated chocolate for your Mint Rocky Road, bear in mind that this melts very quickly, so leaving the chocolate mixture to cool slightly before pouring over your rubble will help to retain large chunks of chocolate instead of feckless little flecks.

BISCOFF CRISPIE SLICE

First things first... tin size. It's up for debate in this recipe, because what it is, is, I've tried to keep everything in this book to a 20cm (8in) square tin (a commendable, pleasant, satisfactory size). Alas, this recipe is trickier to make in small quantities and this marvellous mass is best suited to a whopping 25cm (10in) tin! Having said that, if you don't have a big one to hand, an option is a lined baking tray – use your hand to gently sculpt the mixture into shape.

Second things second – you're gonna need to lube up your hands to best guide and caress this mixture (see tip, opposite). Vegetable oil and a freshly gloved hand are my apparatus of choice (I always have a tub of Crisco and black gloves on me) as the oil is flavourless and the mixture gets extremely sticky!

Prep + hob time: 30 minutes, plus cooling
Serves: 12-16

340g (12oz) mini marshmallows
125g (4½oz) butter
125g (4½oz) golden syrup
50g (2oz) Biscoff spread
275g (9¾oz) puffed rice cereal
75g (2¾oz) smarties, refrigerated

To decorate:
50g (2oz) Biscoff spread
50g (2oz) white chocolate, melted
Biscoff biscuits (optional)

1. Grease and line a 20cm (8in) square cake tin.
2. In a saucepan, melt the mini marshmallows with 100g (3½oz) of the butter over a low heat, stirring often, until viscous and gelatinous.
3. In a second saucepan, melt the remaining 25g (1oz) of butter with the golden syrup.
4. In a third saucepan, melt the Biscoff spread.
5. When everything has melted, pour all the melted ingredients into one bowl and beat quickly to combine. Pour half of the cereal into the mixture and quickly fold through before adding the rest and gently stirring through the sticky mix. Next, add the refrigerated Smarties into the mix and stir through.
6. Pour the mixture into the tin and use a spatula to spread it out until even and squashed into all the nooks and crannies.
7. To decorate, melt the spread in a saucepan before mixing with the melted white chocolate and drizzling over the crispie mix. Chill for 2 hours before removing from the fridge and slicing.

GEORGE LOVES A TIP!

— You can use different spreads and chocolates to make different flavours, including chocolate orange, Nutella, white chocolate – split it into three and make triple chocolate before layering it up. We love, OMG!

— Getting this mixture out of the pan is not the one, quite frankly. Get patient with your spatula, or glove up your hand, douse it in a little veg oil and scrape away.

COCO PUFF CRUNCH SANDWICH

Prep + hob time: 30 minutes, plus chilling
Serves: 6

This is probably the sweetest thing you'll find in this book but I have cravings for these, often! I was trying to make something similar to the cereal bars I'd enjoyed as a child and then stumbled upon too many different recipes for them, so I gave it a go at amalgamating a few to see what worked best. This delicious creation is the result.

For the rounds:
200g (7oz) mini marshmallows
140g (4¾oz) Salted Caramel (see page 28)
125g (4½oz) butter
125g (4½oz) golden syrup
100g (3½oz) chocolate spread
380g (13½oz) puffed rice cereal

For the ganache:
1 quantity of Dark Chocolate Ganache (see page 32)

For the filling:
200g (7oz) Thiccc Caramel (see page 26)

1. Begin with the rounds that'll be the 'bread' of your sandwich. In a large, deep saucepan, melt down the marshmallows with the Salted Caramel (see page 28 for recipe and method) and 75g (2¾oz) of the butter over a low heat, stirring occasionally. This can take up to 30 minutes, but don't be tempted to turn up the heat too high – otherwise you'll burn the mallow mixture! Low and slow is the method here.

2. In a separate saucepan, melt the remaining 50g (2oz) of butter and the golden syrup over a low heat until combined, then in a third saucepan melt your chocolate spread.

3. When all the pans are melted and ready, combine them all into a deep saucepan and stir to combine. It'll be a very sticky gloop but it will come together! Add in the cereal, a third at a time, ensuring that everything is coated before incrementally adding more.

4. When combined, use a 10cm (4in) burger press to create marshmallow-cereal rounds – scoop a couple of tablespoons of mixture into the burger press and gently squash together. Decant the rounds on to parchment paper and set in the fridge for 1 hour. The mixture is enough to make 12 rounds.

5. Follow the method for the dark chocolate ganache on page 32. Next, attach your favourite nozzle to a piping bag and fill with the ganache.

6. Lay out six of the rounds and pipe ganache around the edge of each. Fill the wells in the middle with Thiccc Caramel (see page 26 for recipe and method) before placing another round on top to create your sandwich.

7. Refrigerate for 30 minutes and enjoy!

GEORGE LOVES A TIP!

— Make smaller sweet treats by rolling the coco puff mixture into little balls and refrigerating them until set. The mixture gets sticky as you roll the balls, but a teeny bit of flavourless vegetable oil on your hands will stop you getting into a mess.

SALTED CARAMEL CORNFLAKE MILLIONAIRE'S SLICE

How to make millionaire's shortbread better? Swap out the plain, boring shortbread for a crunchy, salted caramelly, stickathickalicious cornflake layer! Anything cornflake-based is fun to me because of how you can manipulate and handle the caramellow cornflake mixture – I feel like I'm watching one of my favourite TV shows, *Time Team*, because if there's two things I love, it's a dig and a bone.

Prep + hob time:
1 hour, plus chilling
Serves: 12

For the salted caramel cornflake base:
225g (8oz) Salted Caramel (see page 28)
25g (1oz) mini marshmallows
50g (2oz) milk chocolate
175g (6oz) cornflakes

For the caramel layer:
750g (1lb 10oz) of Thiccc Caramel (see page 26)

For the topping:
300g (10½oz) chocolate spread
150g (5¼oz) chocolate, melted

1. Grease and line a 20cm (8in) square cake tin.
2. For your base, start by melting the Salted Caramel (see page 28 for recipe and method), marshmallows and chocolate together in a deep saucepan over a low heat, stirring frequently until gloopy and smooth.
3. Next, add the cornflakes to your mixture a little at a time, tossing and turning until all are glistening and coated. Leave to cool for 5 minutes before turning out into the tin and gently pressing in. Refrigerate for 1 hour.
4. Follow the method on page 26 to make the Thiccc Caramel and leave to cool for 30 minutes before pouring onto the cornflake base. Refrigerate for a further 30 minutes.
5. While your base and caramel cool, make a start on the topping. Melt the chocolate spread in a saucepan over a low heat until smooth. Slowly pour in the melted milk chocolate until combined.
6. Pour on the chocolate topping and decorate with any chocolate you may desire.
7. Refrigerate for 2 hours before slicing up.

GEORGE LOVES A TIP!

— You can top this with anything you like... everybody loves a good topping! I went with white chocolate hazelnut, dark chocolate orange and milk chocolate with Maltesers and Milkybar.

As with all my cornflake recipes, ensure your cornflakes stay crispy and crunchy by always covering them when storing (an airtight container is best). Grab the cheapest cornflakes you can find – the top-shelf versions tend to soak up the caramel and go stale more quickly.

TRIPLE CHOCOLATE CHEESECAKE

Prep + hob time:
30 minutes, plus chilling
Serves: 8

This impressive cheesecake is a doddle to make! Make sure to use a loose-bottomed tin for your cheesecakes though, as springform tins tend to lip the base of your bakes, creating a dented eyesore bigger than a windfarm in a rural village!

For the base:
250g (9oz) chocolate biscuits
125g (4½oz) butter

For the cheesecake:
560g (1lb 3¼oz) cream cheese
375ml (12½fl oz) double cream
100g (3½oz) icing sugar
50g (2oz) white chocolate
50g (2oz) milk chocolate
50g (2oz) dark chocolate

1. Grease and line a 20cm (8in) round cake tin.
2. Now let's get cracking by making the cheesecake base – massacre the biscuits into crumble, melt the butter, combine, and push into the tin. Refrigerate for 1 hour.
3. To make the cheesecake filling, place the cream cheese, 300ml (10fl oz) of the double cream and the icing sugar into a bowl, and whisk until thick, firm and creamy. Divide between three bowls.
4. Melt each of the three chocolates in separate bowls. Add to each bowl one-third (25ml/1fl oz) of the remaining double cream and mix to a ganache. Allow the ganaches to cool before stirring each through one of the three bowls filled with a third of the cheesecake mixture.
5. Remove the base from the fridge and, starting with the dark chocolate cheesecake mix, spread the mixture over the base and smooth the top. Follow with the milk chocolate cheesecake mix, then top with the white chocolate cheesecake mix. Refrigerate for a minimum of 6 hours.

GEORGE LOVES A TIP!

— If you're worried about the neat line between each chocolate layer merging, refrigerate the cake for 5 minutes between adding each layer.

— Want an extra crispy cheesecake base that doesn't crumble as much when cut? Once pushed into the tin, bake the buttery biscuit base in the oven for 5 minutes at 180°C/160°C fan/350°F/Gas 4. Just make sure it cools down before adding any cheesecake filling.

SNICKERS MUNCH

This recipe is mostly a hob job with intervals in the fridge, but very easy to make nonetheless. It's essentially a thinner rocky road with a caramel layer beneath the chocolate topping. You might want to slice these smaller than you would your usual rocky road, as the caramel makes them richer.

We like our rocky road to be solid, chocolate-based and served straight from the fridge. However, if you prefer a bar that's more crumbly and easier to bite into, add 65g (2½oz) of golden syrup to the mix before tossing everything together.

Prep + hob time: 45 minutes, plus chilling
Serves: 15

300g (10½oz) milk chocolate
50g (2oz) butter
125g (4½oz) chocolate spread
100g (3½oz) digestive biscuits
120g (4¼oz) Snickers bars,roughly chopped
75g (2¾oz) mini marshmallows
90g (3¼oz) mini peanut butter cups

For the caramel:
1 quantity of Thiccc Caramel (see page 26)
200g (7oz) Snickers bars, whole

For the topping:
600g (1lb 5oz) chocolate spread
200g (7oz) milk chocolate, melted

1. Grease and line a 20cm (8in) square cake tin.
2. Begin by gently melting the chocolate and butter together over a bain-marie.
3. In a saucepan, melt the chocolate spread.
4. In a large mixing bowl, use a masher to crush the digestive biscuits into an uneven rubble before adding the roughly chopped Snickers, along with the mini marshmallows and mini peanut butter cups.
5. Once melted, pour the chocolate and butter mix into the chocolate spread and stir together before pouring over the rocky road rubble mix. Carefully toss to coat the mix before pouring into the tin and refrigerating for 1 hour.
6. Once set, remove from the fridge and coat with a layer of Thiccc Caramel (see page 26 for recipe and method), before pushing in the Snickers bars in two lines.
7. To make the topping, melt the chocolate spread in a saucepan before adding the melted chocolate and stirring to combine. Pour over the caramel and Snickers layer and smooth out. Refrigerate for 4 hours.

GEORGE LOVES A TIP!

— This is a fun recipe to mix up. It works amazingly with Maltesers – or, if you're looking for an Easter treat, try throwing in 200g (7oz) of Crème Eggs or whatever Easter-themed chocolate you can get your hands on!

— Fancy up the topping by swirling through some melted peanut butter and finishing with a scattering of chopped Snickers bars.

— Remove from the fridge 1 hour before slicing to ensure clean cuts.

— Take note of which way they face so you can slice through them later on for a gloriously nutty cross-section!

COFFEE + WALNUT CHEESECAKE

Despite not being a huge coffee lover, coffee and walnut is one of my favourite flavour combinations. In this cheesecake, a rich, nutty biscuit base perfectly complements the creamy coffee filling.

Back to me! The reason I adore this flavour pairing so much is that it's my favourite bake to make from another author (who just so happens to be my favourite author), Nigella Lawson. I was gifted a copy of *Nigella Christmas* when I was ten, which ignited my love of both baking and Christmas! I'm ostentatiously over the top with both. I buy myself so many presents at Christmas (I deserve them... self-love, etc.) and then tower them up into a grand present fort where I can sit and open my gifts. I'm equally over the top with bakes – I'll do whatever I can to Georgeify a classic bake, cramming puddings within puddings!

Prep + hob time: 15 minutes, plus chilling
Serves: 8

For the cheesecake base:
125g (4½oz) butter
200g (7oz) oat-based biscuits
75g (2¾oz) walnuts

For the cheesecake filling:
560g (1lb 3¾oz) cream cheese
300ml (10fl oz) double cream
125g (4½oz) icing sugar
1 espresso shot, chilled

To decorate:
20g (¾oz) walnuts
Any walnut/coffee-based paraphernalia of your choice (such as Walnut Whips and chocolate-covered coffee beans)

1. Grease and line a 20cm (8in) round cake tin.
2. To make the cheesecake base, begin by browning the butter in a saucepan. To do this, place the butter in a heavy-bottomed saucepan and melt over a medium heat. Allow the butter to bubble away, stirring often, until the butter has foamed, and then turns an amber colour.
3. Blitz, bash and smash together the oat biscuits and walnuts to rough crumbs before mixing with the brown butter and pushing into the tin. Refrigerate for at least 20 minutes while making the cheesecake filling.
4. To make the cheesecake filling, whisk together the cream cheese, double cream and icing sugar until thiccc. With the whisk still running, slowly pour in the chilled coffee and whisk until combined. Dollop the cheesecake filling onto the chilled biscuit base and use a spatula to spread and smooth the top. Cover and chill for at least 4 hours, preferably overnight.
5. To decorate, toast the walnuts in a pan for 3–5 minutes and leave to cool. Pop these onto your cheesecake along with any other walnut or coffee-based treats of your choice.

GEORGE LOVES A TIP!

— I like my cheesecake bases like I like my pâté... coarse. Therefore, my preferred weapon of choice to obliterate my nuts and biscuits is a potato masher! It also comes in extremely handy when pushing the cheesecake base into its tin to create a level base.

CARAMEL CHEW CHEW BARS

I came up with these completely by accident, but now I want to eat these in place of regular chocolate bars daily. I was in a cast pool for the TV game show *The Circle*, which required me to stay in a flat for the best part of three weeks. I had a chaperone for a couple of those, and the only time he asked me to cook something for him was when he wanted to try my Thiccc Caramel. At that point, I was used to stirring huge vats of it, so trying to make a tiny saucepan's worth was throwing me off – I must've been stirring for 30 minutes (far too long!). The end result was so dense that if you were to drop it on the floor it would cause some serious tectonic plate shiftage. A couple years of later and I was lying awake at night still thinking about how embarrassed I was to have made a caramel so thiccc it looked geological, when my mind shifted to stringy caramel and how I could make it work and OMG here we are...

Prep + hob time: 20 minutes, plus chilling
Serves: 10

For the caramel:
150g (5¼oz) butter
130g (4¾oz) light brown sugar
125g (4½oz) golden syrup
600g (1lb 5oz) condensed milk

For the chocolate coating:
400g (14oz) dark chocolate
100g (3½oz) butter
1 tsp salt flakes

1. Grease and line a 20cm (8in) square cake tin leaving the sides uncut.
2. Put all the ingredients for the caramel into a saucepan on a low heat and stir frequently until the sugar has dissolved and the butter has melted. Then turn the heat to medium–high and whisk continuously for 17½ minutes (set a timer!) until the caramel is golden brown and thick. You'll need to keep whisking until you can't whisk no more!
3. Carefully pour the caramel into the tin and leave to set in the fridge overnight.
4. Once set, turn the caramel on to a chopping board, halve it down the middle and slice into 10 long fingers. Melt the chocolate for the coating in the microwave before mixing through the butter until glossy.
5. Use forks to drop the hardened caramels into the chocolate mixture and toss until coated. Place onto a lined baking tray, sprinkle with salt flakes and refrigerate for 20 minutes until the chocolate has set.

GEORGE LOVES A TIP!

— If you like getting a thermometer out, you're looking for around 104–106°C (220–223°F) in step 2.

— On a warm day, freeze the caramel to ensure it firms up and doesn't lose its shape when being enrobed in chocolate.

S'MORES BAR

Prep + hob time:
30 minutes, plus chilling
Serves: 14

The main reason I love s'mores is the excuse to get the blowtorch out and do some charring, but OMG these bars have it all! Crunchy biscuit base, rich, smooth and indulgent chocolate ganache filling and creamy Italian meringue topping with crispy, burned edges.

For the base:
100g (3½oz) digestive biscuits
100g (3½oz) malted milk biscuits
100g (3½oz) butter

For the filling:
225g (8oz) milk chocolate
225g (8oz) dark chocolate
600ml (20fl oz) double cream
75g (2¾oz) icing sugar

½ quantity of Italian meringue (see page 36)

1. For the base, crush the digestives and malted milks to rubble before melting the butter, stirring through and firmly pressing into a lined 20cm (8in) square tin. Refrigerate while making the filling.
2. To make the chocolate filling, melt the chocolates together over a bain-marie. Once melted, take off the heat and beat the double cream through. When it's all incorporated, sieve in the icing sugar and mix through until lump-free. Pour onto the biscuit base and refrigerate for at least 6 hours to set.
3. To make the Italian meringue topping, half the ingredients of the recipe on page 36 and follow the method.
4. Dollop the meringue over the filling and use a fork to make peaks and patterns in the meringue that'll catch when blowtorched. Use a blowtorch (or quickly grill) the meringue until lightly charred.

GEORGE LOVES A TIP!

— Slice up the bar once the chocolate filling has set. Fill up a piping bag with the Italian meringue and use your favourite nozzles to make patterns on top of each bar before scorching individually.

MAKE-IT-YOURSELF CHOCOLATE SLABS

Shop-bought chocolate bars are good and all, but when you can pick your own fillings and stuff giant bakes into them?! You'll never look back! For this recipe you'll have to temper the chocolate to ensure it comes out of the moulds easily, looks glossy and has a nice 'snap' when broken. I always use the seeding method to temper the chocolate, and after a few goes you'll want to stick everything in one of these slabs. You can use different spreads, caramels and sauces to add extra flavour and texture. Just remember that, unless you store the bars in the fridge, the fillings can't be liquid or too runny at room temperature or you'll have oozing, collapsing bars on your hands!

Prep + hob time: 30 minutes, plus chilling
Serves: 3–6

600g (1lb 5oz) white chocolate
240g (8½oz) filling of your choice
Your choice of bake – sliced or crumbled (see step 4)

WHITE CHOCOLATE VARIETY

1. Set aside your moulds. This recipe is based on a mould quantity of roughly 85g (3oz) but if you're opting for a plain design, rather than patterned, 100g (3½oz) moulds would work for this as well.
2. To temper your chocolate, melt 400g (14oz) of the chocolate in a bowl over a bain-marie until it reaches 45°C (113°F). Remove from the heat and add the rest of the chocolate, chopped finely, stirring until it's melted by the rest of the chocolate and reaches 26°C (79°F). Place the chocolate back on the heat and raise the temperature to 28–29°C (82–84°F).
3. To line the bar moulds, place the chocolate in a jug and pour into the moulds, lifting each one up to allow any excess chocolate to drip back into the bowl. Use a scraper or palette knife to clean the tops of the bar moulds before leaving them to set for 5 minutes.
4. You can flavour your bars with a filling and topping of your choice. For a delicious crispy Biscoff variation, top with a serving of my Biscoff Crispie Slice (see page 76) and fill with extra Biscoff spread. Or fruit-it-up by topping with my delicious Cherry Bakewell Cookie Crumble (see page 145) and fill with extra cherry conserve on top. To stuff your moulds, pipe your filling onto the set chocolate, leaving a 5mm (¼in) border around the edges and top with your desired bake.
5. Once the moulds are stuffed, cover with some of the remaining chocolate. If it's set too much and can't be poured, you'll need to heat it again to 45°C (113°F), let it drop off the heat to 26°C (79°F) and then reheat to 28–29°C (82–84°F). Use a palette knife to help seal the slice and filling into the bar with the chocolate.
6. Leave the bar to cool at room temperature for at least 30 minutes before tipping out of the moulds and enjoying! These store best in the fridge but will be absolutely fine at room temperature.

Recipe continues overleaf

600g (1lb 5oz) milk chocolate
240g (8½oz) filling of your choice
Your choice of bake – sliced or crumbled (see step 4)

MILK CHOCOLATE VARIETY

1. Set aside your moulds. This recipe is based on a mould quantity of roughly 85g (3oz) but if you're opting for a plain design, rather than patterned, 100g (3½oz)moulds would work for this as well.

2. To temper your chocolate, melt 400g (14oz) of the chocolate in a bowl over a bain-marie until it reaches 45°C (113°F). Remove from the heat and add the rest of the chocolate, chopped finely, stirring until it's melted by the rest of the chocolate and reaches 27–28°C (81.6–82.5°F). Place the chocolate back on the heat and raise the temperature to 30°C (86°F).

3. To line the bar moulds, place the chocolate in a jug and pour into the moulds, lifting each one up to allow any excess chocolate to drip back into the bowl. Use a scraper/palette knife to clean the tops of the bar moulds before leaving them to set for 5 minutes.

4. Next, pick your flavour. I love topping my milk chocolate slabs with our Cookies + Cream Rocky Road (see page 74) with extra cookies and cream for the filling. Another great option is topping with the Mint Rocky Road (see page 75) and filling with chocolate spread mixed with peppermint extract. To stuff your moulds, pipe your filling onto the set chocolate, leaving a 5mm (¼in) border around the edges and top with your desired bake.

5. Once the moulds are stuffed, cover with some of the remaining chocolate. If it's set too much and can't be poured, you'll need to heat it again to 45°C (113°F), let it drop off the heat to 27–28°C (81.6–82.5°F) and then reheat to 30°C (86°F). Use a palette knife to help seal the slice and filling into the bar with the chocolate.

6. Leave the bar to cool at room temperature for at least 30 minutes before tipping out of the moulds and enjoying! These store best in the fridge if you've got large slices in there but will be absolutely fine at room temperature.

GEORGE LOVES A TIP!

— Before you start lining them with chocolate, use the mould as a guide to slice your fillings to size. You want a slight gap around the edge of the filling so that the chocolate can seal onto the bottom layer.

— You can buy chocolate bar moulds online in all different patterns and styles, but I won't blame you for going with a more simple design as the bars will be less likely to crack coming out.

SALTED CARAMEL CORNFLAKE CREVICE

I'm proper chuffed with this one, not gonna lie. Everyone loves crevice and this one was inspired by a close acquaintance who also provided the stimulus for my bulge recipe! A sticky, salty, sweet cornflake cake, hollowed out, stuffed, brimmed and crammed full of salted caramel sauce and doused in a chocolate topping! They're incredibly fun to make – just make sure you've got strong, dextrous digits.

Prep + hob time:
90 minutes, plus chilling
Serves: 16

For the cornflake cake:
200g (7oz) milk chocolate
100g (3½oz) mini marshmallows
900g (2lb) salted caramel sauce
700g (1lb 9oz) cornflakes

For the filling:
750g (1lb 10oz) Salted Caramel (see page 28)

For the topping:
800g (1lb 12oz) chocolate spread
400g (14oz) dark chocolate

1. Grease and line a 25cm (10in) loose bottomed, square cake tin leaving the sides uncut.
2. To make the cornflake cakes, gently melt the chocolate and marshmallows into the salted caramel sauce over a low heat in a deep saucepan. When the marshmallows have almost melted, beat the mixture with a wooden spoon until it becomes pale and all of the marshmallows have completely melted.
3. Acting fast, pour half of the cornflakes into the mix and gently fold them through the hot caramellow mixture until every cornflake is coated in glimmering caramel.
4. Bit by bit, gently fold through the rest of the cornflakes, making sure not to crush too many in the process. Leave to cool until just warm to the touch, then decant into the tin, gently pushing it down until the surface is even.
5. Now the real fun begins! Using freshly gloved hands, gently make 16 indentations (4 x 4) in your mixture. Then slowly push your dominant finger into each indentation to form holes. Gently ease another digit in, working the cornflake walls up as you go to form crevices ready to be filled with the Salted Caramel. But before that, cool down – put your crevices in the fridge for an hour.
6. Once the cornflake cakes have cooled, fill a piping bag with your Salted Caramel and gently lower your bag into each crevice and fill until it reaches the top. When all crevices are full, refrigerate the tray for 1 hour.
7. To make the topping, slowly melt the chocolate spread in a pan on a low heat while melting the chocolate in the microwave.
8. When the chocolate spread becomes runny, mix in the melted chocolate and, when combined, remove the tray of crevices from the fridge and pour the chocolate mix on top. Aim it at the solid cornflake walls and not the sauce itself. This way there's no chance of chocolate replacing caramel in the holes.
9. Refrigerate the crevices for at least 8 hours, preferably overnight, before slicing into 16 portions.

GEORGE LOVES A TIP!

— To make sure you don't slice into your crevices when cutting, line parchment paper higher up the sides of the tin and use scissors to snip the paper, marking the position of the cornflake walls in the tray. Use these as guides to score the top of the chocolate before cutting into cubes.

— For a less firm, yet richer topping, use chocolate ganache to fill the crevices. This will reduce the shelf life but make for a luxurious crevice!

05

COOKIES + TARTS

Somehow, I've managed to stick together both the quickest and easiest things to make (cookies!) with the, at times, slightly more daunting tarts.

I encourage you to split the tart-making process over a couple of days (your pastry-lined tins will be fine left in the fridge overnight), assembling at the last minute possible to bolster the flavour and ease your stress. While tarts can be more challenging bakes, they're great for when you're in the mood for a slower recipe – and they're all the more satisfying when you eat them! Stuck inside on a rainy, gloomy Sunday morning? Stick on your favourite playlist, film or TV show – have I mentioned, I'm a *Real Housewives* stan? – and get lost in the delight of making the Black Forest Tarts (see page 126) or my twist on a cult classic, the Apple Crumble Tarts (see page 112).

Cookies on the other hand are much more straight forward. Soft. Chewy. Melt-in-your-mouth delicious. Fancy a quick-and-easy treat? Try whipping up a batch of The OG Cookie (see page 119).

What would you like more of? Tarts or cookies? You'll be spoilt for choice with this chapter...

LEMON MERINGUE PIE

What could be more of a crowd pleaser than a zesty tart?! I usually prefer individual tarts to one large one, but there's something so satisfying here about the ridiculously ostentatious ratio of meringue to lemon filling, precariously balanced on a sharp, thinning slice of pie.

This recipe is the perfect amount for the regular-sized tart tin used. But if you like heaps of tart filling like me, go for a deep-dish tin, increase the pastry by 50 per cent and double the lemon filling recipe – you won't regret it!

Prep + baking time:
2 hours
Serves: 6-10

For the pastry:
1 quantity of Super Simple Pastry (see page 40)

For the filling:
50g (2oz) cornflour
175g (6oz) golden caster sugar
Zest of 2 lemons
250ml (8½fl oz) lemon juice
150g (5¼oz) soft butter
6 egg yolks
1 whole egg

For the meringue:
300g (10½oz) golden caster sugar
6 egg whites
1 tsp cream of tartar
2 tbsp cornflour

1. Put a 24.5cm (9½in) round tart tin to one side.
2. To make the pastry, start by mixing the flour, ground almonds and icing sugar together before rubbing in the butter and mixing through the egg yolk and water to form a smooth dough. Chill in the fridge for 30 minutes before rolling out and lining the tart tin. Chill for another 30 minutes before baking. In the meantime, preheat your oven to 210°C/190°C fan/410°F/Gas 6.
3. Blind bake the pastry by lining it with parchment paper filling the bottom of the pastry case with baking beans and baking for 15 minutes. For the second stint of the bake, remove the beans and parchment paper, and cook for a further 5 minutes. Your pastry should be pale but cooked on the bottom.
4. Reduce the oven temperature to 170°C/150°C fan/340°F/Gas 4.
5. To make the filling, mix the cornflour, golden caster sugar and lemon zest in a saucepan before slowly trickling in the lemon juice while whisking to ensure there are no lumps. Place the saucepan on a medium heat and whisk until the mixture becomes very stiff and almost like a paste – this might take a while, but you'll be surprised how quickly it stiffens near the end. Take off the heat, add in the butter and whisk. Next, whisk in the egg yolks and whole egg before returning to the heat for a couple of minutes until the mixture thickens further. Take off the heat and pour the mixture into the pastry case.
6. To make the meringue, place the sugar in a heatproof dish and place in the oven to warm while you whisk your egg whites. When the whites reach soft peaks, remove the sugar from the oven and sprinkle it into the egg whites a tablespoonful at a time, while whisking on a high speed, until combined.
7. When you've added all the sugar, continue whisking, adding the cream of tartar and cornflour until incorporated. It should be really thick and glossy.

Recipe continues overleaf

8. Dollop the meringue around the edges of the tart before filling in the middle and smoothing over the top (if you'd like crispier tops, use a palette knife to spike up the edges of the meringue to form rough peaks). Bake in the oven for 25–30 minutes until golden on top.

9. Leave to cool for 1 hour before removing from the tin and slicing up.

GEORGE LOVES A TIP!

— Adding the warmed sugar to the egg whites helps to stabilize the meringue.

— Spooning meringue onto a warm lemon filling enables the meringue to adhere more easily.

— It's far easier to thicken your lemon filling *before* adding your butter and eggs. Any extra whisking *after* adding them means a greater likelihood of the mixture splitting.

— How do I get it out of the tin so easily? You best believe I'm always using a loose bottomed tin that I can place on a large tin can (I favour my emergency can of organic chickpeas) and leave the sides to fall away while all I gotta do is slide the pie off the base.

— This recipe can also be adapted into mini lemon meringues – simply swap your large tart tin for six 10cm (4in) tins instead and halve the meringue quantity.

WHITE CHOCOLATE RAINBOW COOKIE CUPS

Prep + baking time:
2 hours
Serves: 6

This recipe uses the same tin that we use at the bakery. The tins are the perfect thickness for creating the correct crust: chewy cookie ratio and, my favourite for baking tins only, they're loose bottomed! This recipe is just here to gay up the book a bit. Enjoy!

For the cookie cups:
125g (4½oz) butter
100g (3½oz) light brown sugar
100g (3½oz) caster sugar
2 egg yolks
225g (8oz) plain flour
¼ tsp bicarbonate of soda
½ tsp baking powder
100g (3½oz) white chocolate chips

For the filling:
500g (1lb 2oz) white chocolate
300ml (10fl oz) double cream, room temperature
Oil-based food colouring, as desired
1 quantity of Edible Cookie Dough (see page 34)
Vanilla bean paste
100g (3½oz) white chocolate chips

To decorate:
200g (7oz) white chocolate

1. Preheat your oven to 190°C/170°C fan/375°F/Gas 5. Put aside a tray of 7cm (2¾in) wide x 4.5cm (1¾in) deep heavy-duty dessert tins.

2. To make the cookie cups, cream the butter and sugars together before adding in the egg yolks, flour, bicarbonate of soda and baking powder, mixing until a dough forms. Tip in the white chocolate chips and mix until combined.

3. To fill each cookie cup tin, start by rolling a ball of dough in your hand before squashing it into a disc about 5mm (¼in) thick, and pushing it into the tin. Use more dough to fill any gaps and a knife to trim any excess dough off the top of the tins.

4. Bake in the oven for 12–14 minutes until lightly golden on top. Leave to cool for no more than 2 minutes before using the back of a teaspoon to push any sagging cookie against and up the sides of the tin. This allows it to continue cooking from the tin's residual heat, even as it cools.

5. Leave the cookie cups to cool for another 10–15 minutes before pushing them out of their tins. Use a mini palette knife to tease and coax the cookie cups out of their moulds.

6. Refer to the recipe for Edible Cookie Dough (see page 34) and bake your flour in the oven as described for 8 minutes on a baking tray. Leave to cool until it's just warm to the touch.

7. To make the filling, melt the white chocolate before beating in the room-temperature cream until a thick, glossy ganache forms. Divide into six bowls and mix each with food colouring, as bright as you like.

8. Once the cookie cups have cooled, fill piping bags with each of the ganache colours before piping into each one, working up in rainbow order from violet to red.

Recipe continues overleaf

9. Finish off the remaining steps for the cookie dough topping (see page 34), cream together the butter and brown sugar before sieving in the cooled flour and beating until a dough is formed. Add in the vanilla bean paste, salt and white chocolate chips and mix until evenly incorporated.

10. Use a small ice cream scoop to place balls of dough on the top of each cookie cup. To decorate, melt the white chocolate before drizzling over the cookie cups.

GEORGE LOVES A TIP!

— It's important to get the correct thickness of dough before pushing it into the moulds. If you want a gooey cookie at the bottom, the dough there can be thick. But the sides need to be no more than 5mm (¼in) thick, otherwise the cookie will collapse in the oven and will be hard to repair as it cools.

— If you want to go the extra mile, divide the melted white chocolate for the drizzle of the cookie cups into six bowls, colour each with the rainbow colourings and drizzle a rainbow over the top of each cookie cup as I have!

— As an alternative cookie mould, you can use Yorkshire pudding trays lined with silicone cupcake cases. These may take longer to cook and are best refrigerated once out of the oven and the cases peeled off afterwards.

RASPBERRY + WHITE CHOCOLATE TARTS

Prep + baking time:
1½ hours, plus chilling
Serves: 6

Lots of steps but very simple, fresh and melt-in-your-mouth delicious!

For the white chocolate mousse:
125g (4½oz) white chocolate
40g (1½oz) butter
2 eggs, separated
1 tbsp caster sugar

For the pastry:
200g (7oz) plain flour
30g (1⅛oz) ground almonds
40g (1½oz) icing sugar
125g (4½oz) cold butter, cubed
1 large egg yolk
1 tbsp cold water

For the raspberry jam:
400g (14oz) fresh raspberries
50g (2oz) caster sugar
Juice of half a lemon

For the white chocolate ganache:
200g (7oz) white chocolate
125ml (4¼fl oz) double cream

To decorate:
250g (9oz) fresh raspberries

1. Make your white chocolate mousse by melting the chocolate, butter and 25ml (1fl oz) of water together. Whisk the egg yolks and caster sugar until thick and pale. In a separate bowl, whisk the egg whites to stiff peaks. Pour the melted chocolate and butter mixture into the egg yolks and whisk through. Fold one-third of the egg whites into the chocolate mix to loosen it, before carefully folding through the rest of the whites. Pour into six 3mm (2½in) silicone semi-sphere moulds and chill overnight.
2. To make the pastry, follow the method for Super Simple Pastry (see page 40). Tip on to a work surface and bring together before rolling out to a 5mm (¼in) thickness. Line six 10cm (4in) wide by 3.75cm (1½in) deep fluted tart tins. Chill for 30 minutes and preheat your oven to 210°C/190°C fan/410°F/Gas 6.
3. To blind bake the tart cases, line them with parchment paper and fill with baking beans. Cook for 12 minutes before removing from the oven, taking out the beans and parchment, and returning to the oven for a further 5 minutes. Leave to cool.
4. To make the raspberry jam, tip the raspberries, sugar and lemon juice into a saucepan over a medium heat, stirring often, until everything breaks down and thickens. Leave to cool before spooning into the cooled tart shells and chilling.
5. To make the white chocolate ganache, follow the method on page 32 but melt the white chocolate before stirring through the cream. Pour over the raspberry jam and chill.
6. To finish, remove the white chocolate mousses from the fridge and remove them from their moulds. Place on top of the ganache and use fresh, halved raspberries to decorate.

GEORGE LOVES A TIP!

— The mousses are very heat sensitive, so you may want to freeze them before removing them from their moulds. Place the mousses onto the tarts before decorating, then refrigerate for 30 minutes to allow the mousse to soften.

BLACKCURRANT + ALMOND TART

This recipe seems to convert people because my mum, Lady Jayne, trial baked this for me and kept banging on about how it isn't something she'd eat because she hates blackcurrants. Imagine my surprise when I saw her slicing away at it like she'd just come off a juice cleanse. She was scoffing the lot and 'doesn't even have a sweet tooth', though she takes home kilo tubs of chocolate buttons to eat so I think she must be fibbing! This is a super-easy bake because if Lady Jayne's able to successfully make it, then anyone can perfect it. After all, she's the reason I got into cooking – I couldn't take any more of her meals: turkey stew is a Lady Jayne delicacy...

Prep + baking time: 2 hours
Serves: 12

For the pastry:
150g (5¼oz) plain flour
20g (¾oz) ground almonds
30g (1⅛oz) icing sugar
85g (3oz) cold butter, cubed
1 egg yolk
½ tbsp cold water

For the frangipane filling:
200g (7oz) butter
200g (7oz) caster sugar
4 whole eggs
200g (7oz) ground almonds
400g (14oz) blackcurrant jam (jelly) or conserve

For the icing (optional):
200g (7oz) icing sugar
1½ tbsp cold water
Purple food colouring (as desired)

1. Preheat your oven to 210°C/190°C fan/410°F/Gas 6.
2. To make the pastry, follow the method on page 40. Roll out the pastry to a 5mm (¼in) thickness and line a 20cm (8in) round tin before refrigerating for 30 minutes.
3. Remove the lined tin from the fridge and fill with parchment paper and baking beans. Cook for 15 minutes before removing the beans and parchment paper. Then reduce the oven to 180°C/160°C fan/350°F/Gas 4.
4. To make the frangipane filling, cream together the butter and sugar until light and fluffy – this will take 2–3 minutes. Beat the eggs together and slowly add to the butter and sugar while still mixing until all the eggs have been incorporated. Mix through the ground almonds.
5. To assemble, muddle the jam before spreading over the pastry case. Dollop and smooth over the frangipane filling before baking in the oven for 35 minutes.
6. Leave to cool before icing.
7. To make the icing, mix the icing sugar and water until you have a smooth glaze. Drop 1 tablespoon of the mixture into a bowl and set aside. Pour and spread the rest of the glaze over the tart. Mix the reserved tablespoon with a drop of purple food colouring. Drizzle this in lines over the icing before using a knife or toothpick to feather the purple through the white.

GEORGE LOVES A TIP!

— I've gone with blackcurrant, but you can use whichever flavour of jam you like.

— If you chill the tart for 5 minutes before icing, you'll be much less likely to disturb the frangipane when feathering.

— To muddle your jam, take a teaspoon and mush it around to loosen it in the jar. This makes it easier to spread.

SALTED CARAMEL CHOCOLATE TARTS

Prep + baking time:
1 hour, plus chilling
Serves: 10

Rich, sophisticated, sumptuous... No, not me in an airport lounge trying to pull a rich man, it's my Salted Caramel Chocolate Tart! It requires pretty minimal effort but results in a showstopper packed full of flavour – crumbly, bitter chocolate pastry, sweet salted caramel and a smooth chocolate ganache. You only need a slender slice of this to fill you up and it's perfect for a special occasion!

For the chocolate pastry:
1 quantity of Chocolate Pastry, (see page 40)

For the filling:
500g (1lb 2oz) Salted Caramel, (see page 28)

For the ganache:
1 quantity of Dark Chocolate Ganache, (see page 32)

To decorate:
Salt flakes

1. In a food processor, blitz together the flour, cocoa powder and icing sugar until combined. Add the butter cubes and egg yolk and pulse until a dough starts to form. Slowly add the cold water to help the dough along before turning onto a work surface and bringing together with your hands. Cover and chill in the fridge for 20 minutes.
2. Preheat the oven to 210°C/190°C fan/410°F/Gas 6. Roll out the pastry and line your tart tins. Chill again for 20 minutes.
3. Line a 24.5cm (9in) pastry tin with parchment paper, fill with baking beans and blind bake for 15 minutes before removing from the oven. Remove the beans and parchment paper, and cook for another 5 minutes before leaving to cool.
4. Pour the salted caramel into the cooled tart tin and chill for 30 minutes.
5. Make the ganache by heating the cream on the hob, then pouring it over the finely chopped chocolate. Mix together until you have a silky ganache. Gently pour over the salted caramel filling and chill for at least 2 hours.
6. Remove the tart from its tin, decorate with a sprinkling of salt flakes and serve.

GEORGE LOVES A TIP!

— Setting the salted caramel layer in the fridge should ensure that the ganache doesn't pour into it when spread.

— Use a hot knife to slice through this one and get beautiful layers.

— If your chocolate doesn't melt from when you mix it with the hot cream (step 5), place the ganache bowl over a bain-marie and stir until it comes together.

APPLE CRUMBLE TARTS

I was going through a tart stage, and it was this delicious treat that kicked it off. I kept seeing set caramel and custard tarts on Instagram and I wanted to make something similar with a fun twist that I could devour in a couple of mouthfuls, so I came up with this. Now, judge me all you want, but sometimes I like to double the crumble topping and snack on it like it's granola (it's got nuts, so it's healthy). I only use Bramley apples because they're the tartest, and I like a tart tart.

Prep + baking time:
4 hours
Serves: 6

For the caramel custard domes:
150g (5¼oz) caster sugar
500ml (17fl oz) double cream
¼ tsp ground nutmeg
3 sheets of gelatine

For the pastry:
1 quantity of Super Simple Pastry, (see page 40)

For the stewed apple:
300g (10½oz) Bramley apples, peeled, cored and finely diced
¼ tsp cinnamon

1. Begin by making the caramel custard domes, to allow them plenty of time to set in the fridge. Put the caster sugar into a heavy-bottomed saucepan and melt over a medium heat to create a caramel. In a separate saucepan, gently warm the cream with the nutmeg until steaming. In a bowl, soak the gelatine leaves in cold water.
2. When the sugar has dissolved and turned an amber colour, whisk in the warmed cream followed by the gelatine leaves – make sure you squeeze any excess water out of them before adding. Leave to cool for 5 minutes before straining into 63mm (2½in) silicone semi-sphere moulds and chill on a baking tray in the fridge for at least 4 hours.
3. To make the pastry, follow the method for Super Simple Pastry (see page 40). Tip on to a work surface and bring together before rolling out to a 5mm (¼in) thickness and lining six 10cm (4in) wide by 3.75cm (1½in) deep fluted tart tins. Chill for 30 minutes.
4. Preheat your oven to 200°C/180°C fan/400°F/Gas 6.
5. To stew the apples, place the apples and cinnamon in a saucepan and add a splash of water. Cover and cook on a low heat for 20–30 minutes, stirring often, until a knife easily pushes through a cube of apple. Set aside to cool.
6. To make the egg custard filling, pour the cream, vanilla and nutmeg into a saucepan and heat until steaming. Whisk the egg yolks and caster sugar in a mixing bowl until light and fluffy before whisking in the heated cream mix. Leave to cool.
7. To blind bake the tart cases, line them with parchment paper and fill with baking beans. Cook for 15 minutes before removing from the oven, taking out the beans and parchment, and returning to the oven for a further 5 minutes.
8. Reduce the oven to 160°C/140°C fan/320°F/Gas 3. Spoon a layer of stewed apple into the tart cases, fill with the egg custard and bake for 24 minutes. Leave to cool.

Recipe continues overleaf

For the baked egg custard:

- 250ml (8½fl oz) double cream
- ½ tsp vanilla bean paste
- Pinch of nutmeg
- 4 egg yolks
- 50g (2oz) caster sugar

For the crumble topping:

- 35g (1¼oz) flaked almonds
- 35g (1¼oz) hazelnuts
- 60g (2¼oz) butter, cubed
- 100g (3½oz) plain flour
- 50g (2oz) light brown sugar

9. To make the crumble topping, toast the flaked almonds in a saucepan until lightly browned and fragrant. Roast the hazelnuts in the oven for 15 minutes before putting in a tea towel and rubbing to remove their skins. Roughly chop into halves.

10. Turn the oven back up to 180°C/160°C fan/350°F/Gas 4. Rub the butter into the flour in a mixing bowl before stirring through the brown sugar. Spread over a baking tray and cook for 15 minutes until brown and crispy. Leave to cool. Place the custard domes in the freezer to chill before assembly.

11. To assemble, place a custard dome on top of each custard tart and decorate the edges with the almonds, hazelnuts and crumble mix. Chill for 1 hour before serving.

GEORGE LOVES A TIP!

— You'll likely have a couple of extra caramel custard domes in addition to the six you need, and these just so happen to be delicious sucked on like an ice lolly from the freezer!

COOKIE SANDWICHES

What's a more practicable way to consume cookies faster than by just sticking two of them together?! Efficient and delightful as a larger pudding, cookie sandwiches are such a fun way to add more flavour and texture to an otherwise basic sweet treat. There are varying levels of effort and difficulty here... sticky nougat paired with ganache in the Double Decker + Gold Cookie Sandwiches, a creamier frosting with the Cinnamon Swirl Cookie Sandwiches, and a twist on simple ganache with the Seashell Cookie Sandwiches. Hopefully these also serve as inspiration for some of your own fun, new combinations!

Prep + baking time:
30 minutes, plus chilling
Serves: 5–6

For the cookies:
1 quantity of Edible Cookie Dough (see page 34)
200g (7oz) Double Decker bars, chopped

For the nougat:
1 quantity of Nougat recipe (see page 38)

For the ganache filling:
250g (9oz) caramelised white chocolate (otherwise known as gold chocolate)
150ml (5¼fl oz) double cream

To decorate:
50g (2oz) caramelised white chocolate, melted

DOUBLE DECKER + GOLD COOKIE SANDWICHES

1. Preheat your oven to 190°C/170°C fan/375°F/Gas 5.
2. Make the cookie dough on page 35, but substitute the chocolate chips for chopped up Double Decker bars. Weigh the mixture before dividing and rolling into 12 equal balls. Bake for 10–12 minutes and leave to cool.
3. To make the nougat, begin by creating your syrup. Place the sugar, honey, liquid glucose and water in a saucepan and warm over a medium heat until the sugars dissolve. While the syrup heats, place the egg whites in a clean, dry mixing bowl.
4. Meanwhile, make the ganache by melting the chocolate before beating in cool cream. Place in the fridge to firm up while you finish making the nougat.
5. When the sugars have dissolved, turn the heat up to high and continue boiling the syrup until it reaches 145°C (293°F) degrees. At this point, whisk the egg whites to soft peaks.
6. When the syrup reaches 160°C (320°F), remove it from the heat and steadily pour it into the egg whites while whisking at full speed. The nougat will firm, and the longer you whisk, the firmer it will become. It's best to gradually reduce the speed as the nougat thickens and cools – it will take 2–4 minutes for the nougat to become the perfect consistency.
7. When the gold ganache is firm enough to pipe, fill a bag and pipe around the edges of half the cookies. Transfer the nougat to another piping bag and pump into the middle of the ganache circle before topping with a second cookie.
8. To decorate, quickly drizzle with the melted gold chocolate and chill.

Recipe continues overleaf

Prep + baking time:
30 minutes, plus chilling
Serves: 5–6

For the cookie dough:
150g (5¼oz) butter
80g (3oz) caster sugar
120g (4¼oz) light brown sugar
225g (8oz) plain flour
½ tsp baking powder
¼ tsp bicarbonate of soda
1 tsp cinnamon
2 egg yolks

For the cinnamon filling:
75g (2¾oz) light brown sugar
1½ tsp cinnamon
25ml (1fl oz) boiling water

For the cream cheese frosting:
330g (11½oz) cream cheese
660g (1lb 7¼oz) icing sugar
½ tsp vanilla bean paste

For the caramel filling:
200g (7oz) Thiccc Caramel (see page 26)

CINNAMON SWIRL COOKIE SANDWICHES

1. To make the cookie dough, beat the butter and sugars together. Next, add the flour, baking powder, bicarbonate of soda, cinnamon and egg yolks and beat until a dough forms. Wrap in cling film and chill for 30 minutes.
2. Once cool, lightly flour your surface and roll the cookie dough until it's roughly 5mm (¼in) thick, keeping it in a rectangular shape. It should roughly be 30 x 40cm (12 x 16in) in size.
3. To make the filling, place the brown sugar and cinnamon in a bowl and pour over the boiling water. Stir until a thiccc, cinnamony paste forms and gently spread this over the cookie dough. Next, starting at one of the longer edges, roll up your dough into a long log and chill for 30 minutes.
4. Preheat your oven to 190°C/170°C fan/375°F/Gas 5.
5. Remove the dough from the fridge and slice into 12 equal rounds. Place them, well spaced out, across three baking trays and cook for 11–13 minutes. Once cooked, leave to cool completely.
6. To make the cream cheese frosting, beat the cream cheese until smooth before mixing through the icing sugar and vanilla bean paste until creamy but firm enough to hold its shape.
7. Pipe a round of cream cheese frosting onto half of the cookies before spooning your pre-made thiccc caramel into the centre. Finally top with a second cookie.

Recipe continues overleaf

Prep + baking time:
30 minutes, plus chilling
Serves: 5–6

For the cookies:
150g (5¼oz) butter
80g (3oz) caster sugar
120g (4¼oz) light brown sugar
2 egg yolks
225g (8oz) plain flour
½ tsp baking powder
¼ tsp bicarbonate of soda
200g (7oz) milk chocolate chips
192g (6¾oz) Guylian chocolates

For the ganache and filling:
500g (1lb 2oz) milk chocolate
500g (1lb 2oz) white chocolate
600ml (20fl oz) double cream
300g (10½oz) chocolate hazelnut spread

SEASHELL COOKIE SANDWICHES

1. Preheat your oven to 190°C/170°C fan/375°F/Gas 5. Place the Guylian chocolates in the refrigerator.
2. First up, make the cookies! Cream the butter and sugars together until smooth and fluffy. Add the egg yolks, flour, baking powder and bicarbonate of soda, and mix to form a dough. Tip in the milk chocolate chips and stir through.
3. Weigh the dough before dividing and rolling into 12 equal-sized balls. Space them apart on baking trays before baking for 10–12 minutes until lightly golden on top. Allow to cool for 6 minutes before removing the Guylian chocolates from the fridge and placing three per cookie onto half of all the cookies and allowing to cool further. The other half of the cookies will be the base.
4. Once the cookies have cooled, you can start making two flavours of ganache. Melt the milk and white chocolate in separate bowls before mixing 300ml (10fl oz) of double cream into each. When the ganache is thick, dollop alternating spatulafuls of each into a piping bag fitted with a fluted nozzle tip.
5. Pipe the ganache around the edges of the base cookies (the ones without the chocolates) and watch as the two ganache flavours blend together to emulate the patterns on the chocolates. Fill each of the troughs with dollops of chocolate hazelnut spread before sandwiching with the chocolate-topped cookie. Chill for 30 minutes before serving.

THE OG COOKIE

I think I peaked when I fumbled my way into creating this recipe, because it is the master of all cookies OMG. I first released this cookie recipe in lockdown 1.0 during a drunken bake-along on Instagram, where I kept telling people to add too much baking powder so their cookies wouldn't be as good as mine and they'd still flock back to the market stall post-lockdown. They're incredibly easy to whip up, and balls of the dough can be kept in the freezer to bake from frozen when you need a little pick-me-up! My favourite part of making them is the passive-aggressive drop you give the cookies once they're out of the oven, which gives them the perfect texture.

You'll notice that this recipe crops up a few times throughout the book as a base for other goodies, albeit with a couple of tweaks because it's that damn perfect.

Prep + baking time: 25 minutes
Serves: 11

150g (5¼oz) soft butter
120g (4¼oz) caster sugar
180g (6oz) light brown sugar
2 egg yolks
225g (8oz) plain flour
½ tsp baking powder
¼ tsp bicarbonate of soda
½ tsp salt flakes
200g (7oz) chopped chocolate bars or confectionary

1. Preheat your oven to 190°C/170°C fan/375°F/Gas 5.
2. Cream the butter and sugars together until light and fluffy.
3. Add all of the other ingredients to the mix and beat until a dough forms.
4. Roll the dough into 80g (3oz) balls and space them apart on a baking tray.
5. Bake for 11 minutes until the edges start to turn golden.
6. When taking them out of the oven, lightly drop the baking trays from about 30cm (12in) on to the counter. Leave to cool on their trays for 3–5 minutes before enjoying!

GEORGE LOVES A TIP!

— Mix it up with different chocolate bars and fillings – my favourites are Double Decker bars or, if I'm feeling sensorially overwhelmed, marmite cashews (trust me!).

— Turn these into pistachio perfection by swapping 80g (3oz) of plain flour for the same weight of blitzed pistachios. They pair perfectly with white chocolate chips and the serene seepage of nut oil creates crispier bottoms and edges and a chewy, gooey middle.

THICCC COOKIES

Thiccc Cookies should be gooey in the middle with a crisp shell on top. It's personal preference but, to me, Thiccc Cookies taste best warm! I started playing about more with cookies in lockdown when I still wanted to bake, but needed to easily scale back recipes and just bake what I wanted – cookies are perfect for that. These took a little while to master and you may think the amount of cornflour is ginormous, but it ensures the shape of the cookies and keeps a close texture inside.

Prep time:
30 minutes, plus chilling
Serves: 7–8

200g (7oz) butter
220g (7¾oz) light brown sugar
3 egg yolks
370g (13oz) plain flour plain flour
½ tsp baking powder
½ tsp salt flakes
30g (1⅛oz) cornflour
1 tsp vanilla bean paste
300g (10½oz) milk chocolate chips

MILK CHOCOLATE CHIP

1. Cream together the butter and sugar before adding in the egg and egg yolks.
2. Add the flour, baking powder, salt, cornflour and vanilla bean paste, and beat together before stirring through the chocolate chips.
3. Weigh the dough before dividing and rolling into seven equal-sized balls. Refrigerate for at least 4 hours, or overnight, before baking.
4. Preheat your oven to 180°C/160°C fan/350°F/Gas 4. Remove the cookie balls from the fridge and spread out on lined baking trays, with no more than four on each tray.
5. Bake for 18–20 minutes before allowing to cool – they should retain their shape.

Recipe continues overleaf

Prep + baking time: 30 minutes, plus chilling
Serves: 7

150g (5¼oz) butter
220g (7¾oz) light brown sugar
1 whole egg
2 egg yolks
195g (6¾oz) plain flour
80g (3oz) cocoa powder
½ tsp baking powder
1 tsp vanilla bean paste
½ tsp salt flakes
25g (1oz) cornflour
150g (5¼oz) milk chocolate chips
150g (5¼oz) white chocolate chips

TRIPLE CHOCOLATE CHIP

1. Cream together the butter and sugar before adding the eggs and egg yolks.
2. Add the flour, cocoa powder, baking powder, vanilla bean paste, salt and cornflour and beat together. Add in the chocolate chips and stir through.
3. Weigh the dough before dividing and rolling into seven equal-sized balls. Chill for 4 hours or overnight.
4. Preheat your oven to 200°C/160°C fan/400°F/Gas 6. Remove the cookie balls from the fridge and spread out onto lined baking trays, with no more than four on each tray.
5. Bake for 20 minutes before allowing to cool. They will stoop a little but mostly retain their shape.

Prep + baking time: 30 minutes, plus chilling
Serves: 7

125g (4½oz) butter
100g (3½oz) light brown sugar
120g (4¼oz) caster sugar
3 egg yolks
250g (9oz) plain flour
½ tsp baking powder
½ tsp salt flakes
25g (1oz) cornflour
½ tsp vanilla bean paste
125g (4½oz) pistachios, blitzed and pulverized
300g (10½oz) white chocolate chips

PISTACHIO + WHITE CHOCOLATE CHIP

1. Cream together the butter and sugars before adding the egg and egg yolk.
2. Add the flour, baking powder, salt, cornflour, vanilla bean paste and pistachios and beat together before adding in the chocolate chips. Weigh the dough before dividing and rolling into seven equal-sized balls.
3. Chill the balls for 4 hours or overnight.
4. Preheat your oven to 180°C/160°C fan/350°F/Gas 4. Remove the cookie balls from the fridge and spread out on lined baking trays, with no more than four on each tray.
5. Bake for 20–22 minutes before allowing to cool. They should retain their shape but be golden on top.

Prep + baking time:
30 minutes, plus chilling
Serves: 5–6

For the filling:
200g (7oz) white chocolate hazelnut spread
300g (10½oz) chocolate or filling of your choice

For the cookies:
200g (7oz) butter
220g (7¾oz) light brown sugar
1 whole egg
2 egg yolks
370g (13oz) plain flour
¾ tsp baking powder
½ tsp salt flakes
30g (1⅛oz) cornflour
300g (10½oz) milk chocolate chips
1 tsp vanilla bean paste

STUFFED COOKIES

1. Use a teaspoon or small ice cream scoop to make balls of the white chocolate hazelnut spread, approximately 25g (1oz) each. Place on a lined tray and freeze.
2. To make the cookies, cream together the butter and sugar before adding the egg and egg yolks.
3. Add the flour, baking powder, salt and cornflour, and beat together before adding in the chocolate chips and vanilla bean paste. When dough begins to form, fold in your 300g (10½oz) of chocolate – I like using Kinder chocolates.
4. Weigh the dough before dividing and rolling into eight equal sized balls. Take a ball of dough and wrap it around the frozen spread – repeat until all the dough is used. Place on a lined baking tray and refrigerate for 4 hours or overnight.
5. Preheat your oven to 180°C/160°C fan/350°F/Gas 4. Remove the cookie balls from the fridge and spread out on lined baking trays, with no more than four on each tray.
6. Bake for 20–24 minutes before allowing to cool on their trays – moving them too soon may result in a chocolate spread haemorrhage! The cookies will have flattened a little while cooking but be golden on top.

GEORGE LOVES A TIP!

— Go wild with the Stuffed Cookies recipe – use lemon curd, spreads, jams and conserves, nut butters or whatever you fancy for the filling. You can even use different chocolate bars chopped into the dough to create any flavours you like! Just make sure you give these cookies plenty of time to cool on their trays, then reheat a little before eating.

BLACK FOREST TARTS

Prep time:
4 hours, plus chilling
Serves: 6

Right, now simmer down because this looks like a lot, but I'd recommend you ease yourself into this recipe by making it over a couple of days and just assembling everything at the final step. This is a really satisfying bake: it looks super impressive and tastes sensational! I love the subtle sharpness and vibrant colour of the cherries, and this recipe encapsulates both without being too sweet.

For the mousse:
75g (2¾oz) dark chocolate
50g (2oz) milk chocolate
40g (1½oz) butter
2 eggs, separated
1 tbsp caster sugar

For the jelly:
250ml (8½fl oz) cherry juice
3 leaves of gelatine

For the jam:
250g (9oz) cherries, pitted
75g (2¾oz) caster sugar
juice of half a lemon

For the chocolate pastry:
150g (5¼oz) plain flour
50g (2oz) cocoa powder
15g (½oz) ground almonds
30g (1⅛oz) icing sugar
125g (4½oz) cold butter, cubed
1 egg yolk
2 tbsp of cold water

1. Mousse time! Get started on this by melting the chocolates and butter with 25ml (1fl oz) of boiling water over a bain-marie until smooth. Whisk the egg yolks and caster sugar in one mixing bowl until pale and fluffy. In a second bowl, whisk the egg whites until they form stiff peaks. Gently pour the melted chocolate and butter mix into the egg yolk mix and fold through. Fold a third of the egg whites into the chocolate egg mix to loosen before adding and folding through the rest. Pour into 63mm (2½in) semi-sphere silicone dome moulds and chill in the fridge for 4 hours before moving to a freezer and freezing for a further 1–2 hours.

2. To make the jelly, warm the cherry juice and soak the gelatine leaves in cold water before straining, adding to the warmed juice and whisking to combine. Pour into a lined tray and refrigerate for at least 4 hours.

3. For the jam, put the pitted cherries, sugar and lemon juice in a heavy bottomed saucepan and cook on low for an hour. Stir intermittently, until the sugar has dissolved, the cherries are breaking up and the mixture has thickened. Take off the heat and leave to cool.

4. To make the chocolate pastry, blitz together the flour, ground almonds, cocoa powder and icing sugar in a food processor until fully combined. Add the butter cubes and egg yolks and pulse until a dough starts to form. Slowly add the cold water to help the dough along before turning on to a work surface and bringing together with your hands. Cover and chill in the fridge for 20 minutes.

5. Roll the pastry out and line six 10cm (4in) wide by 3.75cm (1½in) deep fluted tart tins. Refrigerate again for 20 minutes. Preheat the oven to 180°C/160°C fan/350°F/Gas 4.

Recipe continues overleaf

For the cake:
2 whole eggs
2 egg yolks
65g (2½oz) ground almonds
85g (3oz) caster sugar
35g (1¼oz) butter
40g (1½oz) cocoa powder
2 tbsp of cherry brandy

For the ganache:
1 quantity of Dark Chocolate Ganache (see page 32)

To decorate:
6 cherries

6. For the cake, start by whisking the four egg yolks, almonds and caster sugar until pale and fluffy. In a separate bowl, whisk the two egg whites until soft peaks form. Loosen the yolk mixture by folding through one third of the whites before adding the remainder along with the butter and sieving in the cocoa powder while gently folding together. Pour mixture into a lined 20cm (8in) square tin and bake for 8 minutes. Drizzle with two tablespoons of cherry brandy and leave to cool. Turn the oven up to 210°C/190°C fan/410°F/Gas 6 ready for the next step.

7. Line your pastry cases with some greaseproof paper, fill with baking beans and blind bake for 14 minutes. Remove the beans and paper and cook for another 4 minutes before leaving to cool.

8. To assemble, spoon a tablespoon of cherry jam into the cooled pastry case. Use a 7cm (2¾in) round cutter to cut out a piece of cake and place it inside the tart, on top of the jam lining. Use the same cutter to cut a round out of the set jelly and gently transfer it on top of the cake. Remove the mousses from their moulds and place atop the jelly.

9. Make your ganache (see page 32) before piping over and around the mousse, filling the gaps between pastry case and mousse and smoothing out with a spatula. Finish with a fresh cherry on top and refrigerate for 30 minutes before removing from the tart tins.

GEORGE LOVES A TIP!

— Use gloves to pit your cherries so your hands don't turn purple.

— If you want to speed things up a little, just push the pastry into the tart tins as soon as it's made and get straight to cooking it – the texture won't be as flaky though, you have been warned!

— The final assembly is the hardest part of this recipe – just make sure to work quite fast with the ganache so it doesn't set before you've smoothed it on the tarts. Alternatively, use a piping bag with the tip cut off to pipe rounds of more set ganache up the tart. This will seal everything in and create a beautiful pattern.

06

AFTER-DINNER SINNERS

I once attended a Christmas night market in the city of Ely, which is also one of the locations of the regular farmers' market where we pitch a stall on Saturdays. The market was all cute under the lingering, looming presence of the cathedral when all of a sudden, my stall was hit and run by an OAP (Old Age Pillager) on a mobility scooter. Cake went flying, crumbs and curse words were thrown, and I was left clinging for dear life to a near-empty table of bakes, along with a gazebo more bent than I am! I still hear the sounds of the turbo-charged wheels screeching off into the distance and whenever I do, I think of wagon wheels! Giant cookies sandwiched with marshmallow and filling, dunked in oodles of chocolate. They're one of my favourite things to make and there are a few different variations of them in this chapter because I simply couldn't decide on a favourite. They make for a great after-dinner treat when that sweet tooth starts to tingle.

I see some other recipes in this chapter as being particularly festive – although don't let that mean you only make them once a year – Chocolate Hazelnut Mousse Baubles (see page 141) are particularly Christmassy, while the Chocolate Mini Roll (see page 138) can be turned into a delicious yule log. The Strawberry + Champagne Roll (see page 146) also just happens to be my favourite recipe of all time, not just because I went through a good 15 or so bottles of champagne all in the name of recipe testing, but because it's also a quintessential summer spectacle that's perfect for sharing.

WAGON WHEELS

I first made a giant Wagon Wheel (more reminiscent of their original size way back when) a few years ago and it went viral online, which lead to me staying up for nearly two days straight making thousands of them in what is one of the biggest regrets of my life (mostly because I binged the *Twilight* films while plunging fistfuls of cookies into molten chocolate through the night). But I've made it through the wilderness and now love playing around with different Wagon Wheel flavours!

Prep + baking time
3 hours
Serves: 9–10

2 quantities of The OG Cookie (see page 119)

For the marshmallow:
250g (9oz) caster sugar
25g (1oz) liquid glucose
100ml (3½fl oz) water
12g (¼oz) powdered gelatine sachet
100ml (3½fl oz) cool water
1 large egg white (approx. 40g/1½oz)
1 tsp vanilla bean paste

For the ganache:
500g (1lb 2oz) Cadbury Dairy Milk chocolate
300ml (10fl oz) double cream

For the dunk:
800g (1lb 12oz) chocolate spread
750g(1lb 10oz) Cadbury Dairy Milk chocolate, melted

CADBURY'S MILK CHOCOLATE WAGON WHEEL

1. Preheat your oven to 190°C/170°C fan/375°F/Gas 5.
2. To make the cookies, grab your biggest mixing bowl and follow the method on page 119, doubling the recipe. You should have 18–20 cookies – leave to cool.
3. To make the marshmallow, place the caster sugar, liquid glucose and water in a saucepan and boil to reach 115°C (240°F).
4. While your syrup is bubbling away, whisk the powdered gelatine with the cool water and allow to bloom. Place the egg white in a mixing bowl ready to whisk.
5. Meanwhile, make the ganache by following the method in the Back to Basics chapter (see page 32).
6. When the marshmallow syrup reaches 115°C (240°F), start whisking the egg whites to soft peaks on a medium speed. When the syrup reaches 120°C (248°F), remove from the heat and whisk in the gelatine-water mix (it will bubble up slightly so be careful!) before gradually pouring into the egg whites, while whisking.
7. Once all the syrup has been poured in, add the vanilla bean paste and continue whisking, now on a high speed, until thick. This can take a while, but persevere!
8. Once your marshmallow mixture leaves thick ribbons and is warm to the touch, pop it into a piping bag and pipe around the edges of half of the cookies. Fill the middle of the marshmallow circles with the ganache, before sandwiching with another cookie and refrigerating for at least 30 minutes while you make the dunk.
9. To make the dunk, melt the chocolate spread in a saucepan, pour in the melted chocolate and stir to combine. Once fully melted, use two forks to lower, toss and tumble the set Wagon Wheels in the mixture before placing on a lined baking tray and allowing to cool in the fridge for 1 hour until set.

Recipe continues overleaf

Prep + baking time
3 hours
Serves: 9–10

For the shortbread:
400g (14oz) butter
500g (1lb 2oz) plain flour
160g (5½oz) caster sugar

For the marshmallow:
250g (9oz) caster sugar
25g (1oz) liquid glucose
100ml (3½fl oz) water
12g (¼oz) powdered gelatine sachet
100ml (3½fl oz) cool water
1 tsp vanilla bean paste
1 large egg white (approx. 40g/1½oz)

For the filling:
300g (10½oz) Thiccc Caramel (see page 26)

For the dunk:
500g(1lb 2oz) dark chocolate, melted
700g (1lb 9oz) chocolate spread

MILLIONAIRE'S SHORTBREAD WAGON WHEEL

1. Preheat your oven to 180°C/160°C fan/350°F/Gas 4.

2. To make the shortbread dough, rub the butter into the flour until it resembles coarse breadcrumbs before stirring in the sugar and kneading to form a dough.

3. Flour your work surface and a rolling pin then roll out the shortbread until it's 5mm (¼in) thick. Use a 10cm (4in) round cutter to cut rounds out of the shortbread and place on a baking tray. Cook for 15–18 minutes and leave to cool.

4. To make the marshmallow, place the caster sugar, liquid glucose and water in a saucepan and boil to reach 115°C (240°F).

5. While your syrup is bubbling away, whisk the powdered gelatine with the cool water and allow to bloom. Place the egg white in a mixing bowl ready to whisk.

6. Meanwhile, make the Thiccc Caramel (see page 26).

7. When the marshmallow syrup reaches 115°C (240°F), start whisking the egg whites to soft peaks on a medium speed. When the syrup reaches 120°C (248°F), remove from the heat and whisk in the gelatine-water mix (it will bubble up slightly so be careful!) before gradually pouring into the egg whites, while whisking.

8. Once all the syrup has been poured in, add the vanilla bean paste and continue whisking, now on a high speed, until thick.

9. Once your marshmallow mixture cools, pop it into a piping bag and pipe around the edges of half of the cookies. Fill the middle of the marshmallow circles with the ganache before sandwiching with another cookie and refrigerating while you make the dunk.

10. To make the dunk, melt the chocolate spread in a saucepan and pour in the melted chocolate and stir to combine. Once fully melted, use two forks to lower, toss and tumble the set Wagon Wheels in the mix before placing on a lined baking tray and allowing to cool in the fridge for 20 minutes until set.

Prep + baking time
3 hours
Serves: 9–10

For the double chocolate chip cookies:
300g (10½oz) butter
200g (7oz) caster sugar
400g (14oz) light brown sugar
5 egg yolks
375g (13oz) plain flour
75g (2¾oz) cocoa powder
1 tsp baking powder
1 tsp salt flakes
200g (7oz) chocolate chips

For the ganache:
1 quantity of Milk Chocolate Ganache (see page 32)

For the marshmallow:
250g (9oz) caster sugar
25g (1oz) liquid glucose
100ml (3½fl oz) water
12g (¼oz) powd ered gelatine sachet
100ml (3½fl oz) cool water
1 large egg white (approx. 40g/1½oz)
1 tsp vanilla bean paste

For the dunk:
700g (1lb 9oz) white chocolate spread
400g (14oz) white chocolate, melted

To decorate:
50g (2oz) each of white, milk and dark chocolate

TRIPLE CHOCOLATE WAGON WHEEL

1. Preheat your oven to 190°C/170°C fan/375°F/Gas 5. To make the double chocolate chip cookies, follow the method on page 119, adding in your cocoa powder after the plain flour. You should have 18–20 cookies – leave to cool.
2. To make the marshmallow, place the caster sugar, liquid glucose and water in a saucepan and boil to reach 115°C (240°F).
3. While your syrup is bubbling away, whisk the powdered gelatine with the cool water and allow to bloom. Place the egg white in a mixing bowl ready to whisk.
4. Meanwhile, make the ganache by following the method in the Back to Basics chapter (see page 32).
5. When the marshmallow syrup reaches 115°C (240°F), start whisking the egg whites to soft peaks on a medium speed. When the syrup reaches 120°C (248°F), remove from the heat and whisk in the gelatine-water mix (it will bubble up slightly so be careful!) before gradually pouring into the egg whites, while whisking.
6. Once all the syrup has been poured in, add the vanilla bean paste and continue whisking, now on a high speed, until thick.
7. When the marshmallow has cooled, pipe around the edges of half of the cookies. Fill the middle of the cookies with the ganache before sandwiching with another cookie and refrigerating while you make the dunk.
8. To make the dunk, melt the chocolate spread in a saucepan, pour in the melted chocolate and stir to combine. Remove the Wagon Wheels from the fridge and dunk each in the chocolate mix, moving to a lined baking tray when covered in chocolate.
9. To finish, melt the white, milk and dark chocolates and drizzle each over the Wagon Wheels for a triple chocolate topping. Refrigerate for at least 30 minutes before tucking in.

GEORGE LOVES A TIP!

— The Wagon Wheels can be hard to dip if they haven't had long enough in the fridge, so make sure they're firm before tossing.

— If you're struggling to dip the Wagon Wheels with forks, use whatever large utensils you can, or even gloved hands.

— When making your marshmallow, make sure the egg whites are put into squeaky clean bowls, otherwise they won't whisk properly.

CHOCOLATE MINI ROLL

Prep time + baking time: 2 hours
Serves: 7

There's so much fun to be had with this and the best part is... the sponge is fat-free! Yes, there's buttercream and ganache and chocolate, but the fat-free sponge makes it diet-friendly in my eyes...

For the sponge:
6 eggs, separated
125g (4½oz) caster sugar, (25g/1oz extra)
20g (¾oz) plain flour
30g (1⅛oz) cocoa powder
1 tsp icing sugar

For the buttercream:
150g (5¼oz) butter
300g (10½oz) icing sugar
1 tsp vanilla bean paste

For the chocolate ganache:
200g (7oz) milk chocolate
100ml (3½oz) double cream, straight from the fridge

For the chocolate dipping mix:
125g (4½oz) milk chocolate
250g (9oz) chocolate spread

1. Preheat your oven to 180°C/160°C fan/350°F/Gas 4. Grease and line a 30 x 40cm (12 x 16in) baking tray.
2. To make the sponge, place the egg whites into one mixing bowl, then the egg yolks and 125g (4½oz) of caster sugar in another. Whisk the yolks and sugar until thick and pale. Whisk the egg whites, and once at the foaming stage sprinkle in the remaining 25g (1oz) of caster sugar and continue to whisk until soft peaks are formed.
3. Fold one-third of the egg-white mixture into the yolk mixture to loosen it, then gently pour in the rest. Sieve the flour and cocoa powder into the mixture and gently fold everything together so as not to lose any air. Pour your mixture into the baking tray, spread evenly and bake for 12 minutes.
4. As soon as the cake leaves the oven, cut a sheet of parchment paper slightly larger than the size of your tin and sieve a teaspoon of icing sugar on top of the paper to stop the cake from sticking.
5. When you're able to touch the hot cake tin (after about 1–2 minutes), flip the cake out on to the icing-sugar coated parchment paper and carefully peel off the parchment paper it was cooked in. Use the parchment paper on which the cake is now sitting to roll it up into the familiar spiral pattern (the parchment paper can stay in between the cake layers for now). Leave to cool – it only takes 20 minutes.
6. To make the buttercream, beat the butter until softened and add in the icing sugar and vanilla bean paste. Beat until smooth, pale and soft.
7. To make the ganache, see page 32 for the method for heating the chocolate and beating in the cream – you want a thicker ganache so you can roll the cake straight back up in the next step.
8. To assemble the cake, unroll your sponge and spread over the buttercream, followed by the ganache. To roll up the cake, use the parchment paper to help the cake roll into itself, making sure you're now peeling the paper away from the cake as you roll it up. Once rolled, discard the paper and place the cake in the fridge for 30 minutes to 1 hour.

Recipe continues overleaf

9. Trim the edges of the roll before cutting into seven equal pieces. To make the chocolate dipping mix, melt the chocolate before adding to a saucepan of melted chocolate spread. Gently cover each mini roll in the chocolate, leave to set on a wire rack and then refrigerate for 30 minutes until set.

GEORGE LOVES A TIP!

— For a chocolate hazelnut version, replace the ganache or chocolate spread with Nutella, then sprinkle chopped, roasted hazelnuts into the dipping mix for a nut-tastic number!

— Leave the roll uncut, smother in dark chocolate ganache (give it a rough forking!) and get ready to jingle your bells because you've got yourself a yule log, darling.

CHOCOLATE HAZELNUT MOUSSE BAUBLE

Prep + baking time:
2 hours, plus chilling
Serves: 6

To me, these are fancy and decadent, perfect for a dinner party or family celebration, and while some of the elements seem fiddly, they're easy to master! You could just pipe your mousse straight into the silicone moulds without the tempered chocolate linings, but you'd have a tough time dipping them in chocolate and have them set without looking spontaneously combusted. For extra flair, or if you're me and it's a Tuesday, finish with a touch of gold leaf.

For the chocolate hazelnut cores:
100g (3½oz) hazelnuts
100g (3½oz) dark chocolate
35g (1¼oz) icing sugar
½ tsp salt flakes

For the chocolate shells:
200g (7oz) dark chocolate

For the mousse:
225g (8oz) dark chocolate
150g (5¼oz) chocolate hazelnut spread
110g (3¾oz) butter
75ml (2½fl oz) water
6 eggs, separated
2 tbsp caster sugar

For the chocolate hazelnut coating:
500g (1lb 2oz) dark chocolate
75g (2¾oz) chopped roasted hazelnuts

1. Preheat your oven to 200°C/180°C fan/400°F/Gas 6.
2. To make the chocolate hazelnut cores, start by roasting the hazelnuts in the oven for 12 minutes until fragrant before putting in a tea towel and rubbing to remove their skins. Place in a food processor and blitz for 5 minutes until you form a hazelnut butter.
3. Melt the dark chocolate over a bain-marie, then stir through the hazelnut butter bit by bit. Sieve in the icing sugar, add the salt and mix once more.
4. Pipe into twelve 5cm (2in) silicone semi-sphere moulds and chill overnight.
5. To make the chocolate shells, melt the chocolate before pouring into 6.25cm (2.5in) silicone semi-sphere moulds. Use a spoon to pull the chocolate up the sides of the moulds. Tip out any excess before chilling for an hour.
6. Mousse time! Melt the dark chocolate and chocolate hazelnut spread together with the butter and water. Whisk the egg yolks and caster sugar until pale and increased in volume. In a separate bowl, whisk the egg whites to soft peaks.
7. Fold one-quarter of the egg whites into the yolks and sugar mix to loosen it before gently folding through the rest of the whites. Pour the chocolate spread and butter mix down the side of the pan and fold through until incorporated.
8. Delicately remove the chocolate shells from their moulds and pipe mousse into each until full. Remove the chocolate hazelnut cores from their moulds and place onto the centre of each mousse-filled mould before freezing for at least 4 hours.
9. Remove the mousse chocolate semi spheres from the freezer and gently push two halves together to form six balls. Freeze for a further 1 hour.

Recipe continues overleaf

10. To make the coating, temper the dark chocolate (see tip below) and stir through the hazelnuts. Remove the mousse baubles from the freezer and carefully dip and dunk each into the chocolate hazelnut coating until fully covered. Refrigerate for at least 30 minutes.

GEORGE LOVES A TIP!

— Temper your chocolate using the seeding method. Melt 300g (10½oz) of the chocolate in a bowl over a bain-marie until it reaches 50°C (122°F). Remove from the heat and add the rest of the chocolate, finely chopped, stirring until it's melted by the heat of the chocolate and reaches 28°C (82.5°F). Place the chocolate back on the heat and raise the temperature to 32°C (89.5°F).

TIFFIN CUP

Prep + baking time:
1 hour, plus chilling
Serves: 7

As a teenager, I always went for sleepovers with a friend who constantly seemed to have a tray of tiffin ready to consume, and the ingredients were pretty similar to the ones in these Tiffin Cups! Use your favourite milk chocolate to make them extra special, and even add in chopped nuts.

For the tiffin cup case:
600g (1lb 5oz) milk chocolate
60g (2½oz) butter
150g (5¼oz) chocolate spread
100g (3½oz) rich tea biscuits
100g (3½oz) digestive biscuits
100g (3½oz) raisins

For the ganache filling:
1 quantity of Milk Chocolate Ganache (see page 32)

For the topping:
1 quantity of Edible Cookie Dough (see page 34)

To decorate:
80g (3oz) milk chocolate

1. To make the tiffin cup case, start by melting the chocolate and butter together over a bain-marie. Melt the chocolate spread in a saucepan and mix together.
2. Crush the biscuits together into a fine rubble and stir in the raisins. Pour the melted chocolate mixture over the biscuits and raisins, and mix. Dollop the mixture into parchment-lined pudding moulds, 7cm (2¾in) wide x 4.5cm (1¾in) deep, until they're three-quarters full and chill for 45–60 minutes (or until semi-hard).
3. Next, push a blunt shape such as a rolling pin into the chocolate rubble, twisting and applying force to move the mixture up the sides of the mould to create an empty cup in the middle. Chill again for 1 hour until they can be tipped from their moulds and the parchment paper removed.
4. While you're chilling the tiffin cup base, make your edible cookie dough top ping by following the method on page 35.
5. Make the ganache filling, then pour into each of the tiffin cups.
6. To top the tiffin cups, scoop the cookie dough mixture on to each one, then melt the chocolate and drizzle over the top.

CHERRY BAKEWELL COOKIE CRUMBLE

Prep + baking:
1 hour, plus chilling
Serves: 12

Layers of cookie and jam, stacked up, topped with crumble and fused together by baking in the oven – these little slivers of heaven make a change from the generic cookie pie! As always, play about with flavours... I've used everything from plum butter to marzipan.

For the cookie dough:
2 quantities of The OG Cookie (see page 119)

For the filling:
120g (4¼oz) glacé cherries
150g (5¼oz) flaked almonds
800g (1lb 12oz) cherry conserve or jam

For the crumble:
25g (1oz) ground almonds
75g (2¾oz) plain flour
40g (1½oz) butter
40g (1½oz) light brown sugar
15g (½oz) demerara sugar

1. Preheat your oven to 180°C/160°C fan/350°F/Gas 4. Grease and line a 20cm (8in) square, loose bottomed tin.
2. Mix the glacé cherries and flaked almonds into the cookie dough from page 119. You'll be creating a total of four layers. First, push half of the cookie dough into the tin. Top with half of the conserve, then the other half of the cookie dough, and finally the other half of the conserve.
3. To make the crumble topping, mix the ground almonds and flour together, then rub in the butter. Mix through the light brown sugar before sprinkling onto the second layer of cherry conserve. Finish with the demerara sugar.
4. Bake for 40 minutes before cooling at room temperature and chilling for 2 hours before slicing.

GEORGE LOVES A TIP!

— I'm known to detest artificial almond flavouring, but if you want a taste of it, then the best part of the recipe to add it to is into the cookie dough.

— This crumble is amazing warmed up and topped with a scoop of vanilla ice cream!

STRAWBERRY + CHAMPAGNE ROLL

Call me Jennifer Holliday because darling, there was no, no, no, no way I could bash out a baking book and not include at least one recipe laced with alcohol! I spent nearly five years having a daily vintage WKD blue on the rocks (it was an alcohol solution) but, to no one's surprise, you just can't catch that magnificence in a bake.

You don't have to stick with champagne in this recipe if you're not a wannabe upper-middle classhole like me. Sub your champers for rosé, prosecco or, hell, even a Lambrini to make this special, sweet swirl I most associate with a sybaritic summer. A refreshing slice of this would be perfect on a dog-day afternoon; thinking of such makes me want to enjoy a slice with 1970s' Al Pacino (love me that *Serpico* look).

Prep + baking time:
1 hour, plus overnight chilling
Serves: 8

For the jelly:
50g (2oz) caster sugar
100ml (3½fl oz) water
6 gelatine leaves
400ml (13½fl oz) champagne
200g (7oz) strawberries

For the cake:
6 eggs, separated
125g (4½oz) caster sugar, (25g/1oz extra, set aside)
50g (2oz) plain flour
1 tsp icing sugar

For the buttercream:
150g (5¼oz) butter
300g (10½oz) icing sugar
2 tbsp champagne
Red oil-based food colouring, as desired

For the white chocolate ganache:
200g (7oz) white chocolate
100ml (3½fl oz) double cream
Red oil-based food colouring, as desired

1. To make the jelly, start by placing the sugar and water in a saucepan on a medium heat until the sugar has dissolved and the mixture is steaming. Meanwhile, soak the gelatine leaves in cold water.

2. Pour the champagne into a measuring jug. When the sugar syrup is steaming, remove the gelatine leaves from the cold water and squeeze out any excess liquid, then place in the syrup and stir to dissolve. Pour this mixture into the champagne and set aside.

3. Line a 30 x 40cm (12 x 16in) grill pan (you'll also use this for the sponge, to ensure that your jelly and cake are the same size) with several layers of cling film to stop any jelly leakage. For the last cling-film layer, try to use one large piece that's smooth and covers the sides of the pan to stop jelly solution pouring out.

4. To make it easier to roll the dessert later on, slice the strawberries very thinly (2mm/⅛in), then cover the surface of the cling-filmed grill pan with them (I tesselate them as best I can). Place on a shelf in the fridge and very gently pour in the champagne jelly solution. Leave to set for 4 hours or, preferably, overnight.

5. When the jelly has set, use the cling film to carefully lift it out of the grill pan and on to a chopping board large enough to facilitate it, and place back in the fridge. Clean the grill pan and line it with parchment paper. Preheat your oven to 180°C/160°C fan/350°F/Gas 4.

6. To make the cake, place the egg whites into one mixing bowl, then egg yolks and 125g (4½oz) of caster sugar in another. Whisk the yolks and sugar until thick and pale. Whisk the egg whites, and once at the foaming stage sprinkle in the remaining 25g (1oz) of caster sugar and continue to whisk until soft peaks are formed.

Recipe continues overleaf

7. Fold one-third of the egg-white mixture into the yolk mixture to loosen it, before gently pouring in the rest. Next, sieve the flour into your mixture and fold everything together very gently, so as not to lose any air. Pour your mixture on to your lined grill pan, spread evenly and bake for 10–12 minutes until lightly golden on top.

8. As soon as the cake leaves the oven, cut a sheet of parchment paper slightly larger than the size of your tin and sieve a teaspoon of icing sugar on top of the paper to stop the cake from sticking.

9. When you're able to touch the hot cake tin (after about 1–2 minutes), flip the cake out on to the icing-sugar coated parchment paper and carefully peel off the parchment paper it was cooked in. Use the parchment paper on which the cake is now sitting to roll it up into the familiar spiral pattern (the parchment paper can stay in between the cake layers for now). Leave to cool – it only takes 20 minutes.

10. To make the buttercream, beat the butter until softened and add in the icing sugar. Beat until pale and soft. Next, set the mixer to low and slowly drizzle in the champagne. Then add your red food colouring, incorporating it into the buttercream until it is your desired shade.

11. To assemble the cake, unroll your sponge and spread over the buttercream. Lift the jelly out of the fridge and flip it on to the buttercream before peeling off the cling film. To roll up the cake, use the parchment paper to help the cake roll into itself, making sure you're now peeling the paper away from the cake as you roll it up. Once rolled, discard the paper and place the cake on a tray in the fridge to solidify.

12. To make the ganache, see page 32 for the method for heating the white chocolate and beating in the cream. Next, colour your ganache to your likening by adding a few drops of red food colouring. Coat the roll in the ganache and chill for 10 minutes before serving.

SALTED CARAMEL CHOCOLATE FONDANTS

Prep + baking time, 30 minutes, plus chilling
Serves: 10

Not just a dessert that flashy *Masterchef* contestants bake, these salted caramel chocolate fondants are a doddle and you can even keep a spare batch in the freezer! Serve them with some ice cream for a perfectly pretentious pudding.

For the salted caramel cores:
150g (5¼oz) salted caramel

For the batter:
200g (7oz) dark chocolate
225g (8oz) butter
200g (7oz) caster sugar
4 eggs
4 egg yolks
150g (5¼oz) cocoa powder, plus extra, for dusting
50g (2oz) plain flour

1. To make the salted caramel cores, pipe salted caramel into ten 4.5cm (1¾in) silicone hemishere moulds , then freeze for at least 6 hours. If you fancy making your own salted caramel, quarter the recipe on page 28 and follow the method.
2. To help remove your fondants from their moulds later on, refrigerate ten pudding moulds, 8cm (3¼in) wide x 5cm (2in) deep, for 15 minutes before using 25g (1oz) of the butter to grease them right up to the edges. Dust in cocoa powder and tilt the moulds to allow an even dusting all over before returning to the fridge.
3. To make the batter, melt the chocolate and butter together in a bowl over a bain-marie. When melted, whisk the sugar, eggs and egg yolks until extremely thick and significantly increased in volume. Pour in the chocolate and butter mixture and fold through. Sieve in the cocoa powder and flour then fold through once more.
4. Pour the batter into the moulds (about three-quarters full) before refrigerating for at least 2 hours.
5. Preheat your oven to 180°C/160°C fan/350°F/Gas 4.
6. Remove the fondants from the fridge, place onto a baking tray, and use a spoon to make a hole for the core in the middle of each one. Remove the salted caramel cores from the freezer and remove from their moulds. Plop one into each of the fondant holes and cover over by smushing over some fondant batter.
7. Bake in the oven for 15–17 minutes until the tops are cracked and the edges are set. Remove from the oven and, after a minute or so, very gently slide a palette knife between the fondants and their moulds. Once loosened, tip the fondants on to plates and serve.

GEORGE LOVES A TIP!

— If you simply want a chocolate explosion, leave out the salted caramel and bake as soon as the batter is ready. They'll take a couple of minutes less in the oven.

— Keeping the cores frozen while the batter is refrigerating helps balance the cooking times and stop the salted caramel from seeping out.

RASPBERRY + COCONUT MACARON CLUSTERS

Honestly being honest, this recipe doesn't mean a lot to me – though I reckon I could fabricate a story well enough to get me through to an X-Factor judge's house. I am a huge coconut lover though, and that's because when I was 17 and slim I had a sugar daddy friend who was a body builder and convinced me to drink a litre of coconut water a day. Now every time I taste a coconutty concoction, all I think about is Saturday afternoon cheat-day trips to McDonalds and 90s romcoms... fond memories. Do these taste yummabloodalicious though? Hell clucking yes!

Prep + baking time: 30 minutes
Serves: 12

400g (14oz) dessicated coconut
400g (14oz) condensed milk
Pinch of salt
½ tsp vanilla bean paste
2 egg whites
150g (5¼oz) raspberry jam

1. Preheat your oven to 170°C/150°C fan/325°F/Gas 3.
2. Mix together the coconut, condensed milk, salt and vanilla bean paste.
3. Whisk the egg whites in a mixing bowl on high until they reach stiff peaks. Fold through the coconut mixture until all of the coconut is coated.
4. Use a scoop or tablespoon to dollop mounds of the mixture on to a lined baking tray. Wet your thumb and press gently into the top of each mound, re-wetting to stop it getting sticky, to form craters to hold the jam.
5. Muddle the jam to loosen it before using a teaspoon to fill the top of each mound, then bake for 16–18 minutes until golden on top. Leave to cool before removing from the tray and enjoying.

GEORGE LOVES A TIP!

— These catch very easily in the oven, but I find placing a baking tray on a shelf above them prevents them from getting too much colour.

— You can also use a silicone mat on a baking tray (step 4) – the macarons will lift off easily with perfectly cooked and bronzed bottoms.

GOOEY COOKIE BROWNIE PIE

Prep time:
90 minutes, plus chilling
Makes: 12

I'll tell you and warn you right now... you're gonna be doubting me big time on this one, but I promise you that by the end you'll be going back in a hurry for a second slice! The concave pie center is the perfect vessel to serve warm and fill with a scoop of ice cream, doused in chocolate fudge sauce OMG.

For the cookie crust:
150g (5¼oz) butter
150g (5¼oz) light brown sugar
50g (2oz) golden caster sugar
2 egg yolks
225g (8oz) plain flour
¼ tsp bicarbonate of soda
½ tsp baking powder
¼ tsp salt
½ tsp vanilla bean paste
150g (5¼oz) milk chocolate chips

For the brownie filling:
200g (7oz) dark chocolate
250g (9oz) butter
100g (3½oz) caster sugar
4 eggs
200g (7oz) light brown sugar
100g (3½oz) cocoa powder
30g (1⅛oz) plain flour
1 tbsp cornflour
1 tsp salt

1. Preheat your oven to 180°C/160°C fan/350°F/Gas 4.
2. To make the cookie crust, cream together the butter and sugars until pale before adding in the egg yolks, flour, bicarbonate of soda, baking powder, salt and vanilla and mixing to form a dough. Add the chocolate chips and stir through until evenly distributed. Push into a deep 24cm (9½in) tart tin and freeze while making the brownie filling.
3. To make the brownie filling, begin by melting the chocolate and butter together over a bain-marie. Put the eggs and sugars into a mixing bowl and whisk on high until the mixture looks pale and has doubled in size. Gently pour the melted chocolate and butter mixture down the side of the bowl and briefly whisk again. Sieve in the cocoa powder, flour and cornflour, add the salt and stir through.
4. Remove the cookie crust from the freezer and pour in the brownie mixture. Cook for 45–50 minutes until slightly wobbly on top. Leave to cool for 20 minutes before refrigerating to ease its removal from the tin.

GEORGE LOVES A TIP!

— The cookie crust is actually best if frozen overnight before making the next day. Similarly, it's best baked a few hours before you want to eat it – refrigerate the pie until cold, then reheat before eating for ultimate gooeyness!

— When taking the pie out of the oven, it's going to look a state – the crust may have risen and some fallen off and the brownie sinking in the middle, but I promise this is par for the course!

— Check the temperature of the brownie is 89°C (192°F) when cooked.

07

CAKE IT 'TIL YOU MAKE IT

I literally dream of cake. I think about it most often and I'm always conjuring up new flavours, although the ones here are some of my personal favourites and most popular!

At work, I always stay late to bake cakes so I have the whole kitchen to myself. I used to work until 4am icing and decorating cakes while watching some of my favourite comfort films – *Pride & Prejudice*, *Brooklyn*, *Moonlight* ...

When I was in school, I tried to resurrect a cake club whereby each week we'd take it in turns to bake and bring cakes to a lesson. But after infiltrating almost all of my classes and with cake eating increasingly taking precedence over learning – the best type of lesson in my opinion – the cakes were banned. Luckily, real life is less draconian and you can bake every day!

You may've noticed that a few of the cakes in this chapter share a very similar base recipe, and that's because they're modelled on a classic Victoria sandwich cake, for which I would use the three-layer 20cm (8in) cake recipe (see the table below). My intemperance has resulted in a lot of these cakes being sky-scraping spectacles, but it's quite easy to scale cakes up or down. The table will help you work out how to do so!

TIN SIZE / **INGREDIENT**	15cm (6in) x 3 layers OR 20cm (8in) x 2 layers	20cm (8in) x 3 layers	23cm (9in) x 3 layers	25cm (10in) x 3 layers	30cm (12in) x 3 layers
Unsalted butter	200g (7oz)	300g (10½oz)	450g (1lb)	600g (1lb 5oz)	1.2kg (2lb 10oz)
Caster sugar	200g (7oz)	300g (10½oz)	450g (1lb)	600g (1lb 5oz)	1.2kg (2lb 10oz)
Eggs	4	6	9	12	24
Flour	200g (7oz)	300g (10½oz)	450g (1lb)	600g (1lb 5oz)	1.2kg (2lb 10oz)
Baking powder	1 tsp	1½ tsp	2¼ tsp	3 tsp	6 tsp
Butter for buttercream	200g (7oz)	300g (10½oz)	450g (1lb)	600g (1lb 5oz)	1.2kg (2lb 10oz)
Icing sugar	400g (14oz)	600g (1lb 5oz)	900g (2lb)	1.2kg (2lb 10oz)	2.4kg (5lb 5oz)

PISTACHIO, WHITE CHOCOLATE + RASPBERRY CAKE

OMG, I am obsessed with this cake. Two things you should know about me: I love expensive things and anything sweet with nuts – and this bake is a pricey, delightful nut… turned into a cake! It can be transformed into a gluten-free showstopper by simply swapping to a gluten-free plain flour, which is how I always make it. The oils from the pistachios and almonds mean it stays moister than a wet wipe.

Prep + baking time: 2 hours
Serves: 10

For the sponge:
450g (1lb) butter
500g (1lb 2oz) caster sugar
12 eggs
400g (14oz) pistachios, blitzed to a fine powder
300g (10½oz) ground almonds
3 tsp baking powder
75g (2¾oz) plain flour

For the filling:
500g (1lb 2oz) butter
1kg (2lb 3oz) icing sugar
100g (3½oz) white chocolate, melted
350g (12¼oz) raspberries, halved

To decorate:
100g (3½oz) liquid pistachio chocolate (optional – see page 30)
350g (12¼oz) fresh raspberries

1. Preheat your oven to 180°C/160°C fan/350°F/Gas 4. Grease and line five 20cm (8in) round cake tins.
2. Cream the butter and sugar together until light and fluffy.
3. Add the rest of the sponge ingredients and beat until combined.
4. Split between the five cake tins and bake for 25–30 minutes, until a skewer comes out clean and the cake starts to turn golden on top. Leave to cool completely.
5. For the filling, make buttercream by beating the butter until white and fluffy, like a cloud or a prize-winning poodle, then add the icing sugar and beat until even whiter and fluffier. Pour in the melted white chocolate and mix until thoroughly combined.
6. To assemble, layer the cakes with white chocolate buttercream and halved fresh raspberries before carefully coating the sides and top and smoothing with a scraper. If using, pipe the liquid pistachio chocolate down the sides of the cake – or pour on top and use a palette knife to tease it over the edges – before adorning with fresh raspberries.

GEORGE LOVES A TIP!

— At the bakery, we use domestic ovens like yours at home, and can fit up to three cake tins on each shelf.

GALAXY CHEESECAKE CAKE

Prep time: 1½ hours, plus chilling
Serves: 10

Right so what it is, is, this is a delicious chocolate sponge cake, but we're gonna make a cheesecake and smuggle it between the middle cake layers. Texturalizationally (yes, I like making up words), this is incredible! Creamy cheesecake, crunchy biscuit case, fluffy sponge and smooth Galaxy chocolate all coming together, practically combining two desserts in one.

For the sponge:
300g (10½oz) butter
400g (14oz) Galaxy chocolate bar
4 eggs
200ml (6¾fl oz) whole milk
250g (9oz) caster sugar
250g (9oz) self-raising flour
2 tsp baking powder

For the cheesecake:
200g (7oz) biscuits
100g (3½oz) butter, melted
560g (1lb 4oz) full-fat cream cheese,
300ml (10fl oz) double cream
75g (2¾oz) icing sugar

For the ganache:
50g (2oz) Galaxy chocolate bar
25ml (1fl oz) double cream

For the buttercream:
400g (14oz) butter
800g (1lb 12oz) icing sugar
100g (3½oz) Galaxy chocolate bar, melted

1. Preheat your oven to 180°C/160°C fan/350°F/Gas 4. Grease and line five 20cm (8in) round cake tins.
2. We'll make the cheesecake first, as it'll need time to set. Blitz, bash and smash up your chosen biscuits before combining with the melted butter and pushing into one of the cake tins. Set in the fridge while making your cheesecake filling.
3. Next, make a Galaxy ganache by melting the Galaxy chocolate in the microwave until smooth, then stirring through the double cream and leaving aside to cool. Whisk together the cream cheese, double cream and icing sugar on a high speed for 3–5 minutes until thiccc. Add in your Galaxy ganache and beat until incorporated. Dollop onto your now-set biscuit base and smooth over. Chill in the fridge for 4 hours or overnight.
4. To make the sponge, put the butter and chocolate into a bowl and melt over a bain-marie. Beat the eggs and milk together in a measuring jug. When the butter and chocolate mix has melted, add your dry ingredients, eggy milk mix and beat until lump-free. If lumps persist, use a whisk. Divide equally between the remaining four cake tins and bake for 22–25 minutes before allowing to cool.
5. To make the buttercream, beat the butter until soft and add in the icing sugar. When combined, add the melted chocolate and mix until incorporated.
6. OMG this bit's intense but fun, so buckle up. Use the buttercream to sandwich two sponges together. Do the same with the other two cakes, but this time top both pairs off with buttercream and set aside the second pair.
7. Take your cheesecake out of the tin and place it on top of the cakes. Put the second pair of iced cakes on top of the cheesecake (pre-icing them stops you moving the cheesecake too much when icing cakes three and four together). You don't need to use buttercream to stick the cheesecake to the top two cakes, as the cheesecake filling will naturally adhere.

Recipe continues overleaf

For decoration:

- Galaxy chocolate drip (see page 30)
- Galaxy chocolate in any shape or form

8. To seal the cakes and cheesecake with buttercream, use your palette knife to apply the buttercream just to the cake layers, letting excess buttercream hang over the cheesecake in the middle. When the cakes are covered, use some of the remaining buttercream to help the overhanging buttercream from the cakes meet in the middle, over the cheesecake. Don't apply buttercream or pressure directly to the cheesecake – this will just pull the cheesecake from inside the cake and create a buttery cheesecake-y mess!

9. Completely cover the cake with the remaining buttercream and smooth. Leave to set in the fridge for 30 minutes before decorating.

10. To decorate, pipe your Galaxy chocolate drip around the top and finish with a mountain of whatever Galaxy chocolate you can get your hands on.

GEORGE LOVES A TIP!

— Make sure the cheesecake tin and cake tins are the same size.

— Use a potato masher to push the buttery biscuit base of your cheesecake into the tin for a flat, even layer.

— Take the cream cheese out of the fridge 30 minutes before making the cheesecake filling – this will ensure that the Galaxy ganache doesn't immediately solidify when entering the creamy cheesecake filling.

— If you're feeling nervous about icing the cheesecake layer of the cake, add a quick, thin crumb coat of buttercream, then wrap the cake in cling film and chill so that the buttercream seals the cheesecake inside. Remove from the fridge and use the rest of the buttercream to cover the cake once more.

CHOCOLATE TRAY CAKE

The thought of a cake that isn't visually clambering over every other item on a celebration spread makes me shrivel up inside. That said, I'm informed it isn't normal to want to make five-tiered cakes for your birthday every year – even when you have no friends – so this cake's probably for a more laid-back, chill person. The best part of this recipe is that you can pipe buttercream on top, shimmy over some sprinkles and then whip out your calligraphy skills to pipe a message on top (I like something vaguely insulting). Then, when all is consumed and concluded, you can just toss the foil tray away instead of getting all sudsy in the sink.

Prep time: 1 hour plus cooling
Serves: 12

For the sponge:
200ml (6¾fl oz) vegetable oil
100g (3½oz) butter
300g (10½oz) light brown sugar
4 eggs
250ml (8½fl oz) buttermilk
250g (9oz) self-raising flour
100g (3½oz) cocoa powder
1½ tsp baking powder

For the French meringue buttercream:
150g (5¼oz) caster sugar
75ml (2½fl oz) water
8 egg yolks
250g (9oz) butter
1 tsp vanilla bean paste
100g (3½oz) milk chocolate, melted

To decorate:
Sprinkles
Icing writing pens

1. Preheat your oven to 180°C/160°C fan/350°F/Gas 4. Set aside a 32 x 20cm (12½ x 8in) foil tray (no need to line).
2. To make the sponge, beat together the vegetable oil, butter and sugar until creamy before adding in the rest of the ingredients and beating to form a batter.
3. Pour into the foil tray and bake for 26 minutes until a skewer comes out clean. Leave to chill.
4. To make the French meringue buttercream, follow the method on page 41. Then slowly pour the melted chocolate into the meringue mix – make sure the chocolate has cooled right down before doing this – and continue to whisk until incorporated.
5. To help the buttercream thicken after the chocolate is added, chill for 10–20 minutes before smothering all over the cake. Decorate with sprinkles and piped buttercream ruffles, and use an icing writing pen of your choice to add a personalized messages atop!

WHITE LINDT + MILKYBAR MUDSLIDE CAKE

Prep + baking time: 2 hours, plus chilling
Serves: 10

An all-time favourite that has forever graced our market stalls, this cake has two rounds of Milkybar ganache sandwiched between white Lindt truffle cakes. It's a sure-fire crowd pleaser! Think less fluffy Victoria sandwich and more rich pudding slice. This is gorgeous blasted in the microwave for a short interval so that the ganache is molten and the cakes are extra gooey.

For the sponge:
300g (10½oz) butter
200g (7oz) white chocolate
200g (7oz) Lindt Lindor White Chocolate Truffles
4 eggs
200ml (6¾fl oz) whole milk
275g (10oz) caster sugar
250g (9oz) self-raising flour
2 tsp baking powder

For the ganache rounds:
720g (1lb 9oz) Milkybar, finely chopped
600ml (20fl oz) double cream

For the buttercream:
350g (12¼oz) butter
700g (1lb 9oz) icing sugar
100g (3½oz) Milkybar, melted

To decorate:
White Chocolate Drip (see page 30)
White chocolate confectionary to top, as desired

1. Preheat your oven to 180°C/160°C fan/350°F/Gas 4. Grease and line three 20cm (8in) round cake tins.
2. To make the sponge, put the butter, white chocolate and truffles into a bowl and melt over a bain-marie.
3. Beat the eggs and milk together and add to the melted butter and chocolate mixture along with the dry ingredients. Whisk together until combined. Next, split the batter between the three tins and bake for 25–30 minutes, until a skewer comes out clean and the cake starts to turn golden on top. Leave to cool completely.
4. To make the ganache rounds, first grease and line two 20cm (8in) round cake tins (these must be the same size as the three used to bake the sponge), then put the chopped Milkybar into a heatproof bowl. Next, place the double cream in a saucepan over a low heat and gently warm until steaming. Once it begins to steam, pour onto the chopped Milkybar and leave for a minute or two before stirring to completely melt the chocolate. Evenly split your mixture between two cake tins and chill in the fridge until set, ideally for 6 hours.
5. To make the buttercream, mix 350g (12¼oz) of butter , icing sugar and the melted Milkybar until combined. Make sure you let your melted chocolate cool before adding this to the buttercream to prevent it from becoming too sloppy.
6. To assemble the cake, level off your sponges. Apply buttercream to one sponge, top with a round of the set ganache, followed by the second sponge, buttercream, and second round of ganache. Finally, add the last sponge and cover the whole cake in buttercream.
7. Decorate with a white chocolate drip and a tower of white chocolate goodies.

GEORGE LOVES A TIP!

— These cakes are like a cake-blondie hybrid – they are outrageously moist. Take extra care when levelling and stacking them so they don't break.

TIRAMISU CAKE

Prep + baking:
2 hours 30 mins
Serves: 10

I don't like coffee but I'm all over this like Tom Daley is a knitting pattern! I'm certainly not one for *strong* coffee. One Christmas morning, my family thought I needed an ambulance because my heart was palpitating so much – I was freaking out and hyperventilating. It turned out to be the shot of coffee in my morning mug of Kahlua! But by all means, feel free to up the coffee in this cake. All the layers may make this seem daunting but, rest assured – it's super simple.

For the coffee soak:
35g (1¼oz) caster sugar
75ml (2½fl oz) strong coffee

For the sponge:
6 whole eggs
200g (7oz) ground almonds
250g (9oz) caster sugar
6 egg whites
40g (1½oz) cocoa powder
80g (3oz) plain flour
50g (2oz) butter, melted

For the buttercream:
400g (14oz) butter
800g (1lb 12oz) icing sugar
30ml (1fl oz) Marsala wine

For the mascarpone:
250g (9oz) mascarpone
150ml (5¼fl oz) double cream
Cocoa powder, for dusting

For the ganache:
200g (7oz) dark chocolate
125ml (4¼fl oz) double cream

1. Preheat your oven to 180°C/160°C fan/350°F/Gas 4. Grease and line six 20cm (8in) round cake tins.

2. To make the coffee soak, add the caster sugar to the strong coffee and leave to cool.

3. To make the sponge, whisk together your whole eggs, ground almonds and caster sugar until pale, creamy, and doubled in size, then set aside. In a separate bowl, whisk your egg whites until they're forming soft peaks.

4. Use a clean spatula to fold one-quarter of the egg whites into the eggs, almond and sugar mixture to loosen it, then add the rest of the egg whites. Sieve in the cocoa powder and flour, then gently pour the melted butter around the edges of the bowl before carefully folding everything together until you have a smooth, lump-free batter.

5. Divide between the six cake tins and bake for 11–13 minutes, until a skewer comes out clean. Leave to cool completely, then remove from their tins and spoon coffee soak over each layer.

6. To make the buttercream, beat the butter until pale before adding the icing sugar and beating until combined. Gently pour in the Marsala wine and mix.

7. To make the whipped mascarpone, whisk the mascarpone and cream together. Don't over-whip – you do want a little bit of viscosity!

8. Before we start assembly, remember that you need to get five layers out of your mascarpone mix and five layers (plus a coating) out of your buttercream, so don't be too generous! Place one layer of coffee-soaked sponge on your turntable, soak-side up. Spread over a thin layer of buttercream, followed by a layer of whipped mascarpone and a light dusting of cocoa powder. Repeat four more times before finishing with a layer of cake, but place this one soak-side down. Cover with cling film and place in the fridge for 10 minutes to cool and firm up. Once chilled, coat with the remaining buttercream and return to the fridge for 30 minutes to firm up.

Recipe continues overleaf

9. To make the ganache coating, melt the chocolate and add in the cream straight from the fridge to make a thiccc, spreadable substance. Spread it over your fridge-cooled cake. It should set quickly, but if it's a little runny, just pour the ganache on top of the cake and gently tease and spread it down and around the sides as it cools.

GEORGE LOVES A TIP!

— Removing the cakes from their tins before applying the coffee soak means you won't get into a crumby mess while dislodging them. Allow the coffee soak to be absorbed for a good 15 minutes before stacking and icing – this makes it much easier to apply the buttercream.

— Nervous your cake will collapse? Make sure you've got the cling film on hand to quickly, and tightly, wrap up that bad boy and chill until firm and ready to assemble (step 8). Then simply peel away that cake bandage and carry on.

OPTIMAL SURFACE AREA LEMON DRIZZLE CAKE

Prep + baking time:
1 hour 20 minutes
Serves: 6

Yeah, sure, it's a simple and basic recipe but you really can't go wrong with a bit of drizz-drizz. Also, I'm not saying I condone this (read: I absolutely do) but swap out the lemon juice in the syrup for 150ml (5¼fl oz) of limoncello and limon-hello, you've got yourself a winner. FYI, this one-hundred percent counts as one of your five-a-day.

For the sponge:
250g (9oz) butter
250g (9oz) caster sugar
5 eggs, beaten
250g (9oz) self raising flour
Zest of 1 lemon

For the drizzle:
Juice of 3 lemons
150g (5¼oz) caster sugar

1. Preheat your oven to 180°C/160°C fan/350°F/Gas 4. Grease and line a 900g (2lb) loaf tin with deep sides (roughly 7.5cm/3in deep).
2. To make the sponge, cream together the butter and sugar for a decent five minutes until it's so pale and fluffy, it looks almost white.
3. With the mixer still running, slowly pour in the five beaten eggs a little at a time until incorporated.
4. Add the flour and mix until a batter begins to form. Add the zest of one lemon and fold it in with a spatula before dolloping the batter into the loaf tin. Bake for 55–60 minutes or until a skewer comes out clean.
5. Get that drizzle ready for as soon as your cake comes out the oven. To make the drizzle, juice the three lemons and mix with the caster sugar. Spoon two-thirds of the syrup onto the cake and leave it to soak in and crust over. As soon as it's been absorbed, add the remaining third and leave to cool in the tin for 45 minutes before removing and devouring.

GEORGE LOVES A TIP!

— Using a metal loaf tin is always best to achieve optimal citrus sugar crust – the tin retaining its heat means the drizzle will form a crust more quickly, whereas a silicone mould will make for a soggier cake.

— As much as I love a prick, with lemon drizzle, I just pour that syrup on so that the cake stays light and fluffy inside and the edges are crispy and sharp, but if you like insertion then go ahead.

— If your cake's top has domed so much that you're worried the drizzle will pour over the sides of the tin, just add it bit by bit until it's formed a crust and you won't lose any precious citrus.

BANANAPHOBIA CAKE

I have a confession. I have crippling bananaphobia. Yes, that is a phobia of bananas. At one point, I couldn't even look at them or hear the word without an involuntary fight-or-flight response. But, after a long journey of personal growth, I now simply can't tolerate the smell of them, and let me tell you, I can smell one from a couple of hundred metres away. That said, this is another popular bake on the stall – people seem to love the pleasure of having a banana in them. So, I present you with this masterpiece: a cross between a banana bread and a cake.

Prep + bake time:
90 minutes
Serves: 10

For the sponge:
300g (10½oz) butter
150g (5¼oz) caster sugar
150g (5¼oz) light brown sugar
4 eggs
300g (10½oz) self-raising flour
2 tsp baking powder
4 ripe bananas, mushed
100g (3½oz) milk chocolate chips

For the buttercream:
350g (12¼oz) butter
700g (1lb 9oz) icing sugar
30g (1⅛oz) toffee sauce

For the topping:
Banana chips, to decorate
75ml (2½fl oz) double cream, whipped (optional)

1. Preheat your oven to 180°C/160°C fan/350°F/Gas 4. Grease and line two 20cm (8in) round cake tins .
2. To make the sponge, cream the butter and sugars together until fluffy before adding the rest of the cake ingredients (except the chocolate chips) and mixing to form a batter. Fold though the chocolate chips and split between the two cake tins. Bake for 35–40 minutes until a skewer comes out clean. Leave to cool.
3. To make the buttercream, beat the butter and icing sugar together until smooth before adding the toffee sauce (see tip, below) and beating until combined.
4. Slice the cakes in half horizontally, ensuring they're as even and level as possible, to create four fluffy layers. I use a bread knife, but you can get special wire cutters and levellers for cakes if you're feeling fancy.
5. Stack the sponges with a layer of buttercream between each, then coat the outside of the cake with the buttercream. Decorate with banana chips – using piped fluffles of whipped cream to adhere them if desired.

GEORGE LOVES A TIP!

— Make your own toffee sauce by dissolving 50g (2oz) light brown sugar in 100ml (3½fl oz) double cream with 75g (2¾oz) butter and a tablespoon of black treacle. Bring to a simmer before leaving to cool.

— Baking the cake in two layers before slicing to create four means you'll have more fluffy cake and less cake crust.

BLACKBERRY + APPLE CAKE

Prep + baking time:
2 hours
Serves: 10

A fruity autumnal treat, the tangy apples beautifully compliment the tart blackberries in this cake. I like stewing the apples and adding to the cake layers to mix up textures and enhance the flavour. This cake's also a winner because you can just decorate with fresh autumnal blackberries and you're sorted!

For the sponge:
300g (10½oz) butter
225g (8oz) caster sugar
75g (2¾oz) light brown sugar
6 eggs
225g (8oz) self-raising flour
1½ tsp baking powder
75g (2¾oz) ground almonds

For the filling:
6 Bramley apples, peeled, cored and cubed

For the icing:
450g (1lb) butter
900g (2lb) icing sugar
400g (14oz) blackberries

1. Preheat your oven to 180°C/160°C fan/350°F/Gas 4. Grease and line three 20cm (8in) round cake tins.
2. To make the sponge, cream the butter and sugars together until fluffy, before adding the eggs, flour, baking powder and ground almonds and beating to form a batter. Pour equal amounts into the three cake tins and bake for 18–22 minutes until a skewer comes out clean.
3. To make the filling, put the cubed apples into a saucepan with a splash of water, cover with a lid and cook on a low heat for around 25 minutes, stirring often. Once tender, when some of the apple pieces are breaking apart, remove from the heat and leave to cool.
4. To make the icing, beat together the butter and icing sugar until smooth and combined. Obtain the juice from 75g (2¾oz) of the blackberries (I use a metal spoon to squash them through a sieve – no seeds and optimal juice, every time) and beat until incorporated.
5. To assemble your cake, put a quarter of your buttercream into a piping bag and cut a 3cm (1¼in) hole in the end (no need for nozzle nonsense). Ice your first cake layer with a thin layer of buttercream, then pipe a wall of buttercream around the edge of the cake and fill with some of your apple mixture. Place the second cake layer on top, and repeat again.
6. Use the remaining buttercream to coat the sides of the cake. Chill for 30 minutes before decorating with the remaining fresh blackberries.

GEORGE LOVES A TIP!

— The juiced blackberries should add enough colour to the icing but if you want to take it up a notch, squirt a little purple food colouring in there too.

— To up the apple factor, toss a peeled, cored and cubed Bramley apple with a tablespoon of brown sugar and fold through the cake batter for extra juiciness.

BLACK SESAME, CHOCOLATE, COFFEE + CARAMEL CAKE

Prep + baking time: 2 hours
Serves: 10

Now, this one sounds slightly out there but trust me: it's one of the greatest flavour combinations going. It's deep, rich and not too sweet – all the flavours come together perfectly. Also, I'm pretty sure black sesame seeds are a superfood? Health!

For the sponge:
300g (10½oz) butter
300g (10½oz) caster sugar
6 eggs
300g (10½oz) self-raising flour
1½ tsp baking powder
25g (1oz) black sesame seeds, toasted
1 tbsp honey

For the buttercream:
325g (11½oz) butter
650g (1lb 7oz) icing sugar
1 tbsp of salted caramel (see page 28)
2 tbsp strong coffee

For the ganache:
200g (7oz) dark chocolate
125ml (4¼fl oz) double cream

To decorate:
Dark Chocolate Drip (see page 30)
Sesame snaps (optional)

1. Preheat your oven to 180°C/160°C fan/350°F/Gas 4. Grease and line three 20cm (8in) round cake tins.
2. To make the sponge, beat the butter and sugar together until light and fluffy. Add the eggs, flour and baking powder, and mix to form a batter.
3. Blitz the toasted black sesame seeds in a food processor for 30 seconds before adding in the honey to form a smooth paste (you may need to keep scraping down the sides) and adding to the cake batter. Stir through (the batter should turn a speckled black) before dividing between the three cake tins. Bake for 20–22 minutes until a skewer comes out clean. Leave to cool.
4. To make the buttercream, beat the butter and icing sugar together until smooth and creamy. Pour in the salted caramel and coffee and mix until combined.
5. To make the ganache, start by warming the cream in a saucepan over a medium heat until steaming. Pour over the chopped chocolate and leave to stand for 1 minute before stirring together until smooth.
6. To assemble, ice one of the sponges with your buttercream, then spread half of the ganache on top. Stack the next sponge layer on top, spreading with more buttercream and the rest of the ganache. Top this with the last sponge, coating the top and outside in the remaining buttercream. Decorate with a chocolate drip and sesame snaps to finish.

GEORGE LOVES A TIP!

— You can buy ready-toasted black sesame seeds, but toasting your own is easy – just place them in a frying pan over a medium heat until fragrant, then blitz while still warm.

— To grind up the black sesame seeds, the best alternative to a food processor is a pestle and mortar.

— If you're worried your ganache isn't firm enough to ice the outsides of your cake, wrap it in cling film and chill for 20 minutes before finishing off. You'll waste less buttercream bothering with a crumb coat and still get a smooth finish!

S'MORES CAKE

Prep + baking time: 1½ hours
Serves: 10

This cake recipe is my go-to for a quick chocolate cake. The combination of crumbly chocolate cake, crisp biscuits and silky, fluffy and charred meringue is a melt-in-your-mouth treat that makes you pine for autumn, but this can be enjoyed year round.

For the sponge:
225g (8oz) butter
75g (2¾oz) vegetable oil
300g (10½oz) caster sugar
6 eggs
225g (8oz) self-raising flour
75g (2¾oz) cocoa powder
1½ tsp baking powder
150g (5¼oz) digestives biscuits

For the meringue:
300g (10½oz) caster sugar
200ml (6¾fl oz) water
6 egg whites
½ tsp cream of tartar

1. Preheat your oven to 180°C/160°C fan/350°F/Gas 4. Grease and line three 20cm (8in) round cake tins.
2. To make the sponge, cream the butter, oil and sugar together until creamy before adding in the eggs, flour, cocoa powder and baking powder and mixing to form a batter. Divide between the three cake tins and cook for 20–22 minutes until a skewer comes out clean. Leave to cool.
3. To make the Italian meringue, first make a sugar syrup – in a saucepan, dissolve the sugar in the water over a low heat, before turning it up to high and boiling until the mixtures reaches 118–120°C (244–248°F).
4. While your syrup is coming up to temperature, at around 112°C (233°F), whisk your egg whites and cream of tartar until they form soft peaks. As the syrup reaches temperature, slowly pour the sugar syrup into the egg whites while whisking at high speed, and continue whisking once all the syrup is added.
5. Slowly reduce the speed of the whisk as the mixing bowl cools down – it's easiest to work with the meringue while still warm, but it needs to cool down enough to handle and to stop it splitting.
6. When just warm to the touch, you're ready to go! Use the Italian meringue as you would buttercream to stack the three sponge layers together, crumbling the digestives biscuits to your desired coarseness between layers as you go.
7. Finish by covering the cake with the Italian meringue, then scorch the outside of the cake with a blowtorch to your preferred colour.

GEORGE LOVES A TIP!

— You can pick up really affordable blowtorches for your baking kit, meaning you'll always get that authentic charred, caramelized s'mores flavour!

— The Italian meringue recipe is amazingly versatile and can be used as a cheat's topping for Lemon Meringue Pie (see page 102), as decorations for fluffy clouds on a rainbow cake or to make a quick s'mores traybake (see page 90).

— The cake is also delicious baked in a 23cm (9in) square tray and eaten warm.

BISCOFF + CARAMEL CAKE

Prep + baking time:
3 hours
Serves: 16–20

This cake is the epitome of showstopping cake brilliance! It's a sky-scraping concoction of caramel that's so large you're gonna need to serve it on platters and chopping boards! Baking Biscoff spread into the cake batter makes for an even lighter, fluffier cake, while the thin layers of caramel not only help the cake layers adhere but will make you salivate, too!

Before you get started, pop on your favourite calming playlist, whack on a film or, if you're partial to one, pour yourself a stiff drink because this is a MEGA bake.

For the sponge:
450g (1lb) butter
450g (1lb) caster sugar
9 eggs
450g (1lb) self-raising flour
2 ¼ tsp baking powder
50g (2oz) Biscoff spread

For the buttercream:
300g (10½oz) sticky caramel (see tip overleaf)
600g (1lb 5oz) butter
1.2kg icing sugar (2lb 10oz)
100g (3½oz) Biscoff spread

To decorate:
300g (10½oz) Biscoff spread
100g (3½oz) Biscoff biscuits

1. Preheat your oven to 180°C/160°C fan/350°F/Gas 4. Grease and line four 20cm (8in) round cake tins.
2. To make the sponge, beat the butter and sugar together until light and fluffy. Chuck in the eggs, flour and baking powder, and mix until combined. Then add the Biscoff spread and keep on mixing briefly until incorporated (too much mixing can result in a less-than-fluffy sponge). Divide the batter between the four cake tins and bake for 25–30 minutes.
3. To make the buttercream, beat the butter and Biscoff spread together until smooth, then add the icing sugar until you've got what is essentially cake cement that tastes absolutely delicious (go on, have a little try). You can add a splash of milk if required to smooth out the buttercream, but you want to build a big, bulging beauty, so solid foundations are crucial.
4. Slice the cooled cakes in half horizontally, ensuring they're as even and level as possible. I just use a bread knife but you can also get special wire cutters and levellers for cakes.
5. Making sure you've got cling film to hand, start the stacking. Spread buttercream then caramel over the first sponge layer, top with the second sponge then continue until you're reaching the stars. Wrap cling film around your monolith immediately and house in the fridge until firm enough to finish. Cover your remaining buttercream while it chills.
6. When stable and sturdy (after about 1 hour), remove the cake from the fridge and use the remaining buttercream to ice the sides. Smooth and chill again while you prepare to decorate.

Recipe continues overleaf

7. Melt 100g (3½oz) of Biscoff spread in a saucepan until drippable, then pipe or tease the molten Biscoff down the sides of your cake. It should set as it drips down the chilled buttercream.

8. Arrange dollops, blobs and globules of the remaining 200g (7oz) of thiccc Biscoff spread onto the cake and adorn to your fancy with Biscoff biscuits.

GEORGE LOVES A TIP!

— Panic not – these sponges will take longer to cook because they're deeper, and adding Biscoff spread to the batter seems to increase the cooking time. But the cakes always turn out miraculously moist and delicious.

— To avoid a leaning, lopsided erection, I lay all of the sponges out, spread buttercream across all but one (for the top) first, then add caramel between each layer as I stack them. It reduces drag when constructing the cake and decreases your chances of collapsy-wapsy woe.

— Salted caramel sauce (see page 28) will do as the caramel layer, but make sure it's been chilled to the desired spreadability.

OREO BROWNIE CAKE

Prep + baking time: 3 hours
Serves: 12

When it comes to Oreos, one thing's for sure – a double stuffing is optimal. The creme filling is far superior to the enveloping cookies, and the ratio of creme to cookie in this variety is bang on. For the decorating, I like to get my hands on as much Oreo paraphernalia as possible. I'm talking Oreo double-stuffed cookies, Oreo chocolate brownie cookies, Cadbury Dairy Milk Oreo bars, Milka Oreo bars – the list goes on... Have fun with this one and go wild!

For the brownie layers:

400g (14oz) milk chocolate
500g (1lb 2oz) butter
500g (1lb 2oz) caster sugar
160g (5½oz) cocoa powder
130g (4½oz) plain flour
8 eggs
4 x 157g (5½oz) packs of double stuffed Oreos

For the icing:

2 x 157g (5½oz) packs of double stuffed Oreo's
280g (9¾oz) cream cheese, softened
120g (4¼oz) butter
1kg (2lb 3oz) icing sugar

For the chocolate drip:

1 quantity of Milk Chocolate Drip, see page 30

1. Preheat the oven to 180°C/160°C fan/350°F/Gas 4. Grease and line four 20cm (8in) round cake tins.
2. To make the brownie layers, melt the chocolate and butter together in a bowl over a bain-marie. Once melted, add the dry ingredients and the eggs, then beat together until smooth and divide between the four cake tins. Gently push one pack of Oreos into the batter in each tin and cover completely with displaced batter. Bake the brownies in the oven for 18–22 minutes until an inserted thermometer reaches 89°C (192°F).
3. Let the brownies cool for 5 minutes at room temperature before refrigerating for at least 2 hours to achieve a fudgy texture.
4. To make the icing, use a knife to split the remaining Oreos. Scrape the creme filling into one bowl and put the biscuit halves to one side. Add the cream cheese and butter to the creme filling and beat until smooth. Add the icing sugar and beat until you have a smooth, creamy icing.
5. Blitz the dry Oreo biscuits in a food processor (or you can pop them in a food bag and bash them with a rolling pin) until you have a crumby consistency with no large chunks remaining. Add them to your icing and mix through.
6. Let's get cracking on this cake stacking! Stack your chilled Oreo brownies, smoothing a layer of icing between each. Then coat the outside with the icing, smoothing with a scraper as best you can (any larger chunks of biscuit may tug along the way).
7. Decorate with a chocolate drip and Oreo-adjacent confectionary.

GEORGE LOVES A TIP!

— It's important to separate the Oreos despite using all parts of them in the icing. If you chuck them in whole you won't have a creamy frosting, but a lumpy, bumpy mix instead, and ain't nobody wanna spread that!

— In step 4, remove the cream cheese from the fridge 30 minutes before using to ensure it doesn't solidify the butter when mixing.

— If your icing is a little sloppy, add some more icing sugar and mix well.

VANILLA RAINBOW CAKE

Prep + bake time: 1½ hours
Serves: 12

I'mma get it off my chest now – I don't think putting vanilla into actual cakes does a damn thing! My top tip here to maximize the taste of the vanilla is to pop it into the buttercream instead to really bring out its flavour. For this recipe, I'd recommend using vanilla extract (or if you're feeling extra fancy and in the mood for a little splurge, try vanilla bean paste, which I swear by) because vanilla essence is made from *beaver butts*. Yup, beavers secrete a vanilla-tasting substance that someone has licked, enjoyed, bottled and sold. Don't say I never teach you anything. Now for the recipe...

For the sponge:
450g (1lb) butter
450g (1lb) caster sugar
9 eggs
450g (1lb) self-raising flour
2 ¼ tsp baking powder
Food colouring in rainbow shades, as desired

For the buttercream:
600g (1lb 5oz) butter
1.2kg (2lb 10oz) icing sugar
1 ½ tsp of vanilla bean paste

1. Preheat your oven to 180°C/160°C fan/350°F/Gas 4. Grease and line six 20cm (8in) round cake tins.
2. To make the sponge, cream together the butter and sugar until fluffy. Add in the eggs, flour and baking powder, and mix to form a batter.
3. Weigh the batter and divide equally between six mixing bowls. Colour each portion with your chosen food colouring and stir.
4. Pour each bowl of coloured batter into its own cake tin, then bake in the oven for 16–18 minutes. You should expect slightly thinner layers for this recipe that won't take too long to bake. Leave to cool.
5. To make the buttercream, beat the butter and icing sugar together until smooth, then add the vanilla bean paste (or extract) and mix until incorporated.
6. Let's get those cakes stacking! Level off your cakes to ensure your stack doesn't lean. I always go purple upward but each to their own – just remember that 'Richard of York Gave Battle In Vain' for the order (but indigo and violet really are the same thing so you only need one purple layer). Spread buttercream between each of the sponge layers before covering the final layer with even more buttercream and smoothing.
7. At the bakery, we like to use any excess buttercream to ruffle the top and finish with little rainbow fizzy belts, but you know what? Just do whatever tickles your pickle. Have fun with this recipe!

GEORGE LOVES A TIP!

— Overmixing your batter will hinder the rise of the cake, as you'll overwork the gluten. So when adding the colours into the batter, use a spatula to fold them through instead of a food mixer and beating the living daylights out of them like you're starring in a *Rocky* sequel.

CHERRY BAKEWELL CAKE

A cult classic at the bakery, I've taken this beauty to every market, and it sells out every time. I make it gluten-free for markets – see the tip for how overleaf. Also (soz to make it all about me but this is my book so what it is, is) I'm really not a fan of almond essence. Something about the smell sets me right off on a sensory spiral! But, if it appeals to you, add a drop of almond essence to your tart filling for an extra almondy kick. I won't judge you, I promise.

Prep + baking time:
3 hours
Serves: 10

For the tart pastry:
200g (7oz) plain flour
35g (1¼oz) icing sugar
75g (2¾oz) butter, cold and cubed
1 egg yolk
1 tbsp cold water

For the filling:
150g (5¼oz) butter
150g (5¼oz) caster sugar
3 eggs
150g (5¼oz) ground almonds
400g (14oz) cherry conserve (save 75g/2¾oz for assembly)

For the sponge:
300g (10½oz) butter
300g (10½oz) icing sugar
6 eggs
200g (7oz) self-raising flour
100g (3½oz) ground almonds
1½ tsp baking powder

For the buttercream:
350g (12¼oz) butter
700g (1lb 9oz) icing sugar
½ tsp cherry flavouring
Red oil-based food colouring, as desired

1. Preheat your oven to 210°C/190°C fan/410°F/Gas 6. Set aside a 20cm (8in) round tart tin, and grease and line two 20cm (8in) round cake tins.
2. To make the pastry, start by mixing the flour and icing sugar together before rubbing in the cold butter with your fingers and mixing through the egg yolk and water to form a smooth dough. Chill in the fridge for 15 minutes before rolling out to line the tart tin. Trim and chill for another 30 minutes.
3. To make the filling, start by creaming your butter and sugar together until smooth before adding the eggs and ground almonds, and mixing some more.
4. Blind bake the pastry by lining with parchment paper, filling with baking beans and baking for 15 minutes. Remove from the oven, take out the beans and parchment paper, and bake again for 5 minutes.
5. Reduce the oven temperature to 180°C/160°C fan/350°F/Gas 4. Spread all but 75g (2¾oz) of cherry conserve onto the pastry base then dollop on the filling, gently spreading for even coverage (avoid pulling up the jam below). Bake for 40–50 minutes until set with just a slight jiggle, and leave to cool.
6. To make the sponge, cream the butter and sugar together until light and fluffy before adding the eggs, flour, ground almonds and baking powder. Beat until a batter is formed and divide between the two cake tins. Bake for 30–35 minutes until a skewer comes out clean. Leave to cool.
7. To make the buttercream, beat the butter and icing sugar together, add cherry flavouring to taste and a drizzle of red food colouring. Then on a chopping board, cut 2cm (¾in) from the outside edge of the tart and keep the cut-off crust aside for decoration.
8. To assemble the cake, place about a third of the buttercream onto one of the sponges, followed by the Bakewell tart. Smear the remaining cherry conserve over the top of the Bakewell tart to adhere the second sponge layer on top. Use the remaining buttercream to coat the cake and leave to set.

Recipe continues overleaf

9. Decorate with Bakewell tart offcuts and other cherry-related paraphernalia of your choice.

GEORGE LOVES A TIP!

— If you're having trouble getting your pastry to bind, add in the leftover egg white and chill it for longer to make it easier to manage when rolling.

— The natural oils from the ground almonds will keep the cakes nice and moist.

— Gluten-free-ify the cake by swapping the flour in the pastry and sponge for gluten-free flour and it's that simple!

MAPLE SYRUP + BACON CAKE

I prefer cake to American-style pancakes, therefore, this has happened*. Essentially, it's an Americanized Victoria sandwich cake, I suppose. Use the best quality bacon you can and make sure you're using sturdy, meaty rashers for optimal structure. You're probably thinking about taking five minutes to get your head around this one, but just remember – life is a succession of five-minute moments so (not to be the Dalai Drama) you need to get on with things or you'll end up with more regrets than a *Celebrity Big Brother* ejectee.

*Following that logic, this is a breakfast food!

Prep + baking time: 1½ hours
Serves: 10

For the sponge:
300g (10½oz) butter
300g (10½oz) caster sugar
6 eggs
300g (10½oz) self-raising flour
1½ tsp baking powder
1 tbsp maple syrup

For the buttercream:
300g (10½oz) butter
600g (1lb 5oz) icing sugar
1 tbsp maple syrup

For the maple-candied bacon:
500g (1lb 2oz) maple-cured bacon
75g (2¾oz) light brown sugar
250ml (8½fl oz) maple syrup

1. Preheat your oven to 180°C/160°C fan/350°F/Gas 4. Grease and line three 20cm (8in) round cake tins.
2. To make the sponge, cream together the butter and sugar until light and fluffy. Add in the eggs, flour and baking powder, and mix to form a batter. Add in the maple syrup and stir through. Pour into the three cake tins and bake for 20–22 minutes until a skewer comes out clean. Leave to cool.
3. To make the buttercream, beat the butter until pale and fluffy before adding in the icing sugar. When combined, pour in the maple syrup and beat again.
4. Stack up the sponges with a layers of buttercream and coat the outsides *before* candying the bacon – the buttercream needs to 'set' for the bacon to adhere.
5. To candy the bacon, lay the rashers out in a grill pan before sprinkling with the brown sugar and drizzling over the maple syrup. Bake at 180°C/160°C fan/350°F/Gas 4 for 20–25 minutes until golden and caramelized, with the bacon crispy in some places and chewy like jerky in others.
6. When cool enough to touch but warm enough to peel away from the rack (see tip, below), stick the rashers of candied bacon to the buttercreamed sides of the cake before enjoying!

GEORGE LOVES A TIP!

— Make this cake even more audacious by using maple bacon butter as the basis of your buttercream. Place two rashers of candied bacon in a food processor and blitz to dust before adding in the butter and pulsing to combine, then add the icing sugar as usual.

— Timing is everything with candied bacon. Pick them off the grill pan too soon and you'll burn your digits, but leave it too long and it'll stick to the grill pan instead of the cake!

COOKIES, CREAM + EVERYTHING IN-BETWEEN CAKE

Fluffy cake, crispy, chewy cookies and chocolate chip cookie-dough balls all layered up to create a cookie centerpiece. I've been working on this recipe for a little while in the kitchen: it was originally a cake covered in cookie-dough-flavoured icing with a giant cookie-dough wrap. Then, I took it a step further and topped it with crispy, chewy cookies until it slowly snowballed into a cacophony of everything on the cookie spectrum!

Prep + baking time:
2 hours
Serves: 12

For the sponge:
125g (4½oz) butter
350g (12¼oz) caster sugar
5 eggs
350g (12¼oz) plain flour
360ml (12¼fl oz) buttermilk
2 tsp baking powder
100g (3½oz) milk chocolate chips

For the cookie layers:
1 quantity of The OG Cookie (see page 119)

For the frosting:
2 x 157g (5½oz) packs of double stuffed Oreos
160g (5½oz) cream cheese
150g (5¼oz) butter
800g (1lb 12oz) icing sugar

To decorate:
1 quantity of Milk Chocolate Drip (see page 30)
1 quantity of Edible Cookie Dough (see page 34)
Oreos and/or cookies of your choice

1. Preheat your oven to 190°C/170°C fan/375°F/Gas 5. Grease and line three 20cm (8in) round cake tins.
2. To make the sponge, cream the butter and sugar together until pale and fluffy – there's a lot more sugar than butter here, but remember to trust the process!
3. Add the rest of the ingredients (apart from the chocolate chips) and mix until you have a smooth batter – it will be more liquidy than your average cake batter.
4. Fold the chocolate chips into the batter and divide between the three cake tins. Bake for 20–22 minutes, until a skewer comes out clean and the sponge is springy to touch.
5. To make the cookie layers, divide the dough between two 20cm (8in) round cake tins (you will have some dough left over for a rainy day!). Bake for 14 minutes until the edges start to turn golden, then drop onto a wire rack to keep them gooey and leave to cool.
6. To make the frosting, use a knife to split the Oreos and scrape out the creme filling and put into a bowl. Put the biscuits in another bowl and set aside. Add the cream cheese and butter to the creme filling and beat until smooth. Then add the icing sugar and beat again until smooth.
7. Crush the reserved Oreo biscuits with a masher to a coarse, uneven rubble, and fold this through the frosting.

Recipe continues overleaf

8. To assemble the cake, layer one quarter of the frosting on to one of the sponges, smooth out and top with one of the large cookie rounds. Repeat with another layer of cake and cookie (don't apply frosting to the cookies) and finish with the third layer of cake.

9. Use the remaining half of the frosting to coat the cake, and then decorate with a chocolate drip, Oreos, mini chocolate chip cookies and cookie-dough balls.

GEORGE LOVES A TIP!

— Make sure your cream cheese has been brought to room temperature before mixing the frosting to avoid the butter becoming lumpy.

— Don't be tempted to skip the step of separating your Oreos! If you do, you'll end up with a clumpy, lumpy mixture that won't be texturally sound.

— Add chocolate ganache (see page 32) or a cookie milk soak to the cakes for more decadent, special-occasion bakes.

— To make a cookie soak, heat an oven to 180°C/160°C fan/350°F/Gas 4. and bake 45g (1¼oz) double-stuffed Oreo cookies for three and a half minutes, until warm and gooey. Soak in 200ml (6¾fl oz) whole milk along with 1 tbsp caster sugar for 15 minutes before straining.

INDEX

D

E

F

G

H

I

J

K

L

M

T

U

V

W

UK/US GLOSSARY

Baking tray = baking sheet
Bicarbonate soda = baking soda
Caster sugar = superfine sugar
Cling film = plastic wrap
Cornflour = cornstarch
Dark chocolate = semi-sweet chocolate
Demerara sugar = turbinado sugar
Double cream = heavy cream
Glacé cherries = maraschino cherries
Icing sugar = confectioner's (or powdered) sugar
Jam = jelly
Jelly = jello
Jug = pitcher
Kitchen roll = paper towel
Measuring jug = measuring cup
Parchment paper = baking paper
Piping bag = pastry bag
Piping nozzle = piping tip
Plain flour = all-purpose flour
Self-raising flour = self-rising flour
Sieve = strainer
Sprinkles = hundreds and thousands
Tea towel = dish towel

I recommend using the measurements listed in the individual recipes but here's a nifty little conversion chart if you need to check your measurements at any stage.

CONVERSION TABLE

Metric	Imperial
15g	½oz
20g	¾oz
25g	1oz
30g	1⅛oz
35g	1¼oz
40g	1½oz
55g	2oz
60g	2¼oz
75g	2¾oz
80g	3oz
90g	3¼oz
100g	3½oz
115g	4oz
120g	4¼oz
125g	4½oz
150g	5¼oz
175g	6oz
200g	7oz
225g	8oz
250g	9oz
275g	10oz
300g	10½oz
325g	11½oz
350g	12¼oz
375g	13oz
400g	14oz
450g	1lb
500g	1lb 2oz
550g	1lb 3oz
600g	1lb 5oz
650g	1lb 7oz
700g	1lb 9oz
750g	1lb 10oz
800g	lb 12oz
850g	1lb 14oz
900g	2lb
1kg	2lb 3oz
1.2kg	2lb 10oz

OVEN TEMPERATURES

°C	Fan °C	°F	Gas Mark
120	100	250	½
140	120	275	1
150	130	300	2
160	140	325	3
180	160	350	4
190	170	375	5
200	180	400	6
220	200	425	7
230	210	450	8
240	220	475	9

VOLUME

Metric	Imperial
25ml	1fl oz
50ml	2fl oz
75ml	2½fl oz
100ml	3½fl oz
125ml	4¼fl oz
150ml	5¼fl oz (¼pint)
200ml	6¾fl oz
225ml	7½fl oz
250ml	8½fl oz
300ml	10fl oz (½pint)
350ml	12 fl oz
375ml	12½fl oz
400ml	13¼fl oz
450ml	15fl oz/¾ pint
500ml	17fl oz
600ml	1 pint/20fl oz
700ml	23½fl oz / 1¼pints
800ml	27fl oz
900ml	31½fl oz /1½pints
1 litre	35fl oz /1¾pints

ACKNOWLEDGEMENTS

Lemme tell you something, this whole thing was nearly a giant lesson in hubris OMG.

A huge thank you to Zoe and Olivia for making this possible for me.

For the incredible photography, Kimberly, I can't thank you enough and explain how in awe I am! Thank you for opening up your home to Samantha and I. Katie, thank you for your beautiful styling, laughs and hands. I need not be so nervous watching you slice and decorate – and your utility belt makes Batman look inadequate.

To my editor, Nicole, for keeping me on track, talking me down when needed and encouraging me so enthusiastically. I could not have finished this without your guidance – thank you!

Thank you to my bakery babes for constantly evolving how you work and churning out my new ideas with minimal moan.

Samantha, for so effortlessly making me look amazing at all times, you're everything I could hope for in a sister (and so much less!). There are so many sides to you – market stall server, sugary snack concocter, white van man, qualified first aider, cinematographer, constant headache, wedding-jam runner and I appreciate every single one. You juggle it very well!

To those closest to me, thank you for putting up with my stress levels, diva-like tendencies, frantic phone calls and hours upon hours of nonsensical voice notes. I'm a cross between Malcolm Tucker and Logan Roy at the best of times and this amplified that exponentially.

Finally, to my parents, I know I'll never be favourite but at least I'm God. Thank you for always helping me stay on track and gifting me with so much of your time and space. I wouldn't have achieved any of this without you. I'm forever grateful and will cherish the memories forever.

Oh, and also to me for somehow pulling this off. Where there's a gay, there's a way!

First published in Great Britain in 2024 by

Greenfinch
An imprint of Quercus Editions Ltd
Carmelite House
50 Victoria Embankment
London EC4Y 0DZ

An Hachette UK company

A CIP catalogue record for this book is available from the British Library

HB ISBN 978-1-52943-145-2
eBook ISBN 978-1-52943-146-9

10 9 8 7 6 5 4 3 2 1

Commissioning Editor: Nicole Thomas
Designer: Studio Polka
Photography: Kimberly Espinel
Food styling: Katie Marshall

Printed and bound in China

MIX
Paper | Supporting responsible forestry
FSC® C008047

Papers used by Greenfinch are from well-managed forests and other responsible sources.